54 SIMPLE TRUTHS WITH BRUTAL ADVICE:

How to Face the Challenges of Life

54 SIMPLE TRUTHS WITH BRUTAL ADVICE:

How to Face the Challenges of Life

2nd Edition

Michael Wash

Illustrated by Tessa Hall with contributions from Ben Johnson

First edition published in Great Britain by MWA Publications © Michael Wash, 2007. Michael Wash has asserted his right under the Copyright, Designs and Patents Act 1988 to be identified as the author of the book. A CIP record for this book is available from the British Library.

ISBN 9780953644810

Second edition published in Great Britain by Michael Wash through www.lulu.com.

ISBN 978-0-9536448-4-1

A CIP record for this book is available from the British Library.

To those of you who find the courage to read this book and discover a way of living with your own truth.

Foreword

In this unique book, Mike Wash shares a wealth of personal wisdom drawn from real-life experiences. The examples come from a variety of contexts, including home, leisure, and work. Mike has worked in health, education, and business settings. He tells impressively honest stories of gain and loss, of celebration and suffering, of joy and regret, and of achievement and failure. In the telling of these 'truths,' we find the inspiration to reflect upon the rich tapestry of our own lives: our values, beliefs, relationships, choices, decisions, failures, successes, hopes, and dreams.

This book gives plenty of information and ideas, but more than that, it gives the reader hope – the hope that can lead to an honest reappraisal of our own experiences and the confidence to be the person we most want to be.

Who would benefit from this book? Anyone who wants to make the most of his or her life and learn about living!

Dr Mary Connor, co-author, *Coaching & Mentoring at Work,* London: Open University Press, 2007

**This book is linked to a self help community website
www.54-self-help-books.com**

Further book review comments

"This book takes life realistically by the horns and encourages us to live life to the full. It covers some extremely valuable insights which will resonate with all of us who want to understand ourselves better, and are courageous enough to listen to brutal truths. In support of the Simple Truths, Mike shares the wisdom learned through his personal and professional experience for us to chew on as we will."

Dr Graham Dexter and Dr Janice Russell authors of Introduction to Coaching (Sage 2010) www.healthandlifetransitions.com

"The 54 simple truths are brutal, stark, blunt, honest .... but dealt with a guiding hand that seeks to support us to be the best we are and can be. Interestingly, after reading I also feel kinder and more open to others. They too are coping with life's simple truths and I can be patient of that. This book gives me a sense of calm without removing the fact that life can be tricky"

Lindsey Jackson Life Coach and Director of Enhance.

Preface to the Second Edition

The first edition has evoked strong reactions, mostly positive (it also gained recognition as a shortlist winner of the USA Book News Award in 2008); however, feedback indicates that some of the original illustrations were a little too challenging and that each simple truth left readers wanting to know more. I have therefore changed most of the illustrations and added to each chapter. Most of the stories used to illustrate the simple truths are based on personal experience and/or inspired by others I know although some of the names of the individuals have been changed to protect their privacy.

The illustrations are by Tessa Hall; some are based on original ideas by Ben Johnson from the first edition. Samples of Ben's work from the first edition can be seen in chapters 13, 21, 24, and 45.

About Michael Wash

At the age of fifteen, after spending eighteen months in a Catholic school, training for a life of a religious teacher as a De La Salle brother, I decided to come home and face the realities of a different type of family life. The desire within me to help others was still strong, and on the eve of me leaving to do voluntary services overseas at the age of seventeen, an opportunity to join the school of psychiatry as a student nurse was too much of a coincidence to ignore.

Those first few years working in a large mental institution in the early 1970s, wiped out any sense of remaining naivety or innocence I had about the capability of the human mind to destroy itself and others. My path was set, but I was unhappy to be constrained by 'institutional walls,' so after psychiatry, I trained as a general nurse, then as a tutor – and in my private practice, qualified as a counsellor and psychotherapist.

The constraining nature of the 'health' profession was still too much, so I decided to explore outside. My horizon changed significantly when after writing a paper proposing that most senior managers suffer from organisational psychoses or neurosis, I was offered a job in a large telecommunications company. Here, I introduced counselling as a legitimate form of support for the business and the value of developing a supportive, 'facilitative change management' style of leadership. My premise was that large organisations damage your health – and it doesn't have to be that way.

The irony was that during this time, I battled for six months against cancer, which created a greater strength and determination in me to carry on the path of 'healing,' whether in the context of work or family life. During these very formative years, I also experienced the tragic death of my mother. Following an accident, she was left in a coma for several years. Also, my little sister fell ill and endured years of kidney dialysis before succumbing to hepatitis and kidney failure. As a trained nurse I was able to support her on home dialysis for several years.

I was married young, and one of the proudest moments of my life was witnessing the birth of my twin sons. The strain of tragedy, illness, and personal change was too much for my marriage, and divorce eventually cut the chains – enabling us both to be free and to find new happiness.

I have been running my own business for the past twenty years and feel very privileged to have worked with people and organisations passionate about wanting to change and discover their true potential. I am very happy, married to Mave, and enjoying my grandfather status and the attention of my sons and stepchildren. The journey continues...

Acknowledgements

To my wife, Mave, for her honest, loving companionship and support.

To George Buchanan, for his brutal but professional feedback. To Dr Mary Connor, Lindsey Jackson, and Dr Niamh Leonard, for their constructive feedback and support.

To Dr Graham Dexter and Dr Janice Russell for their confidence and support in my endeavours.

To Bel Mooney and Sue Quilliam, two nationally recognised relationship advisors who were kind enough to review and recommend this simple text.

Finally, to Deepak Chopra, an author of great wisdom and spirit who has helped me consolidate the connections between mind, body, and soul.

Contents

Introduction

Life is very short, and some people go through life learning very little or not realising that experiences coming their way are inevitable. The simple truths you are about to read are those inevitable events, incidents, and moments that will touch everyone eventually in his or her lifetime. We can make the most of the time we have by being alert and aware of the choices we make in life and the impact they have on ourselves and others.

Exploring, debating, and reflecting on these simple truths may raise complexities and 'grey' areas, and you may say that there is no such thing as a simple truth.

What may be a truth for some may not be for others. What is simple to some is complex to others. The point here is – it's your choice. You choose what value you gain from these reflective and challenging statements. Challenging, because each simple truth is accompanied by 'brutal' advice. Brutal, only in the sense that I have not included any complex, theoretical, or academic reasoning behind what I write here. Instead I have chosen the path of tough love, to get straight to the point leaving you with personal reflections and challenges and I hope, a desire to find out more through the many self help resources available.

I have tried to express the ideas from the heart with good intention so that when you pause and ask yourself "so what?" the answer is in the realm of common sense or some will find the answers difficult to accept. By the way, a word of warning: always be wary of advice given to you. It's always better to take your own counsel, make your own choices, and forge your own direction. I hope you enjoy the journey you are about to embark upon, and perhaps you may add other simple truths to the 54 described here.

After you read, I hope you take the opportunity to share your experiences and insights on our self-help community website. Join our stimulating and insightful community. Read about other people's life challenges and how they deal with them. Share your own. Find more help with health, weight, stress and business success. We also have forums for teachers, parents and students.

www.54-self-help-books.com.

'Truth is like a vast tree, which yields more and more fruit the more you nurture it. The deeper the search in the mine of truth, the richer the discovery of the gems buried there, in the shape of openings or an ever greater variety of service.'

—Gandhi

'Most of our struggles in life are resistance to truth. We struggle to make our truth the Truth – to undo or redo the past. We squirm and have anxiety over the future.… Aligning your truth with the Truth will enable you to live out your purpose and experience the thrill of the present moment.'

—Deepak Chopra

'No matter how hard its adversary – falsehood – may try to overwhelm it, truth refuses to yield. I am prepared to stand by the truth, even if everyone is against me.'

—Nelson Mandela

'From the viewpoint of absolute truth, what we feel and experience in our ordinary daily life is all delusion.… If we can realise and meditate on ultimate truth, it will cleanse our impurities of mind and thus eradicate the sense of discrimination. This will help to create true love for one another. The search for ultimate truth is, therefore, vitally important.'

—Dalai Lama

'Never apologise for showing feeling. When you do so, you apologise for the truth.'

—Benjamin Disraeli

'Whoever is careless with the truth in small matters cannot be trusted with important matters.'

—Albert Einstein

I know the truth - give up all other truths!
No need for people anywhere on earth to struggle.
Look - it is evening, look, it is nearly night:
what do you speak of, poets, lovers, generals?
The wind is level now, the earth is wet with dew,
the storm of stars in the sky will turn to quiet.
And soon all of us will sleep under the earth, we
who never let each other sleep above it.

—Marina Tsvetaeva,

1. There will always be a sunset and a sunrise – you can't hold back time.

Life is not a rehearsal; live for now! Don't live in the past – it's gone! Fine, have happy memories, but don't dwell on what was bad or what might have been. Another thing: the future hasn't happened yet, so don't worry about it. The future is in your imagination, so by all means be excited and positive about what's possible – but don't screw yourself up with fear of the unknown. Worrying about the past and the future will stop you experiencing the moment – now!

Of course, time is precious, but time is only something we humans have invented to measure the days passing. What's more important is how we choose to spend that time. Don't tell me you never have enough time – there's always enough time. What matters is how you choose to prioritise what's important to you.

Are you spending too much time at work? Must be more important than spending time at home, then! Getting stressed at work or working long hours? It must be more important than your health, then! Upset about lines on your face and grey hair? Losing what you've had must be more important than what you've got, then!

How old are you? Never mind. Whatever your age, that age is special to you; celebrate it. Throughout life, we experience different things, and that experience is partly dependent on age and maturity. So what you are right now is perfect – enjoy it! Whenever you see a sunrise, wonder what surprise or miracle will happen today. When you see a sunset, be thankful for what is, right now!

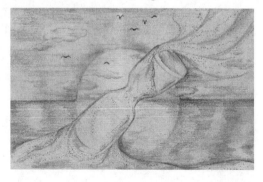

Although David's anger and frustration were now well imprinted onto the steering wheel, his face was becoming less contorted and red. He was now resigned to being late for a crucial business meeting that would, potentially, secure him more work. Eventually the traffic began to resemble a stop-start moving chain of connected vehicles, all anxious to rekindle the sense of getting somewhere fast. It had been one hour and seven minutes since David had moved, and no matter how much reorganising of diaries, he knew deep down that this was a big deal. The situation was not helped by the drivel on the radio and a traffic update thirty minutes ago saying the road had cleared! It was obviously a serious accident, given the number of sirens and flashing blue lights reminding others to put things in perspective. Once David's anger subsided, it gave him time to reflect. He wondered what his wife shouted to him as he was rushing out this morning. He hadn't had time to say 'good-bye' or 'I love you.'

He was also thinking that he hadn't seen his children for a few weeks because it had been a particularly busy period at work. He also felt a tinge of guilt for not returning two calls from his now rapidly aging mother.

As David passed the scene of the accident, he had the usual thoughts of 'why do people slow down to have a look at the carnage?' However, it was a particularly nasty-looking crash. As David cautiously accelerated away, with a shiver down his back, he wondered what the chances were of having two identical cars with identical number plates. Could the driver-licensing department really make that sort of mistake?

'The grand show is eternal. It is always sunrise somewhere; the dew is never dried all at once; a shower is forever falling; vapour is ever rising. Eternal sunrise, eternal dawn and gloaming, on sea and continents and islands, each in its turn, as the round Earth rolls.'

—John Muir

2.   Death is inevitable.

You are going to die. Death is part of life! Some people are so frightened of dying that they become the walking dead. They avoid anything they perceive as a risk: trains, planes, motorways, the outdoors.

If you think about it, we have died several times already. Where's the baby you? The five-year-old, the ten-year-old, the teenager? They exist only in memory .Our whole body changes about every five years. Every cell is renewed, we enter different phases, new strengths emerge as old strengths decay.

Why face this aspect of life? Because making it nondiscussable or not facing it can prevent you from experiencing a good death, either for yourself or a loved one. Some people's fear of death or fear of the process of dying or not wanting to face their mortality prevents them being with loved ones who are dying. The last moments with a loved one will stay with you for the rest of your life; you can make this good or traumatic. Whilst you are alive, you can influence this by having a say in how you want to die. Make a living will, and tell your loved ones what you want. It may be the last and kindest gift you give them.

Some people believe that this is not the end – that we are born again into another life. Whatever your beliefs, our body dies and our spirit and soul may live on. We can't prevent death but nor should we fear it. Now, once you have found the courage to face up to the inevitable, tick the box! Move on, and enjoy what's left!

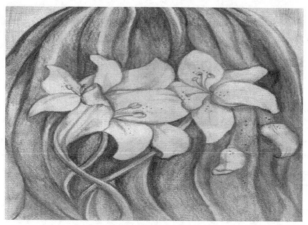

Mary was exhausted and drained, yet satisfied and calm now that she had seen all her close family and friends and told them what she wanted during her last few days of life. At thirty-five, and with her eight-year-old daughter and five-year-old son, it was particularly harrowing to realise that she wouldn't live to see their next birthdays.

Her dear and devoted husband had not left her side since she was admitted to the hospice, and he had worked very hard to prepare for Mary coming home to be with her family in her last days. The final ten days of life, apart from the last two days when she slipped into a coma, were indeed, as she said herself, some of the best days of her short but beautiful life. To have all her friends and family around her and to talk openly about the love, meaning, and value of what they all had together was an experience everybody would carry with them. No doubt it would enrich their own final days.

Mary's message to everyone was to not look back but to look forward. Don't fear things that may or may not happen, and today, tell someone you love him or her and mean it deeply.

One of the last things Mary did was to hand over the personal 'love' bags she had made for her children. In these were photos, a letter, and one or two small, precious items related to the time the children had with their mum.

Mary's funeral was, down to the smallest detail, exactly what she wanted. Everyone said that her spirit was evident in every word and every act. Today her spirit continues to live on, and all those who had been a part of her life and her death remember her short life with love, joy, and gratitude.

'For what is it to die, but to stand naked in the wind and melt into the sun.'

—Khalil Gibran, from *The Prophet*

3.   You have the power to choose.

If you ever feel sorry for yourself, look around. There are many more people worse off than you, and most of them have found the courage to carry on and make the most of what they've got.

Don't be passive or a victim in this life…you can choose what and how to be. We may not be able to control or prevent certain events, but we can choose how to react to them. Many people underestimate their personal power and quickly fall into a dependent relationship with someone, or in some extreme cases, everyone. They become powerless and feel victimised and communicate in terms of 'oh, poor me' or 'life's not fair.'

What they don't realise is that they have responded or reacted rather than choosing to influence the situation or the way they feel about it. It doesn't have to be like this. You can choose to be happy, healthy, and successful. You can choose to change the way you feel about your life or situation or even change your life! OK, so what about the down-and-outs and the homeless? Somewhere on the way, they made choices that got them there. They now need help rediscovering their power.

What about the mentally ill? Don't underestimate their power to choose within what may be a different view of the world. What about the differently abled? We can learn about real power from those who have chosen to shift from *disabled* to *specially abled*! What about the persecuted and tortured, the survivors of disaster? History shows that the survivors somehow chose not to give in; they chose to fight on and made a decision with determination to live.

What do you want to do? It's your choice!

Sheena was bubbling over with such excitement that she disclosed to strangers at her friend's birthday party, without hesitation, her relief at long last that her fiancé has asked her to get married. They were going to San Francisco and would do it in style and have the greatest time of their lives.

Two weeks before the happy couple was due to leave, Sheena had a relapse and her multiple sclerosis was to strike its most bitter blow yet. Within a week, Sheena was paralysed from the neck down. What was her future to be now? Keeping positive and hoping for another remission became increasingly difficult as the months dragged on.

Eventually, Sheena was allowed home. Wheelchair-bound, with some movement in her arms, she now faced a very different future than the one in which she dreamed of marriage in San Francisco. Unfortunately, her relationship with her fiancé deteriorated, and they agreed to split up. This set of circumstances would be enough to depress anyone, but not Sheena.

As her friend I visited regularly, and it was a delight to be in her company. She chose to be positive, to laugh and joke about the silliest of things – whether it was a catheter getting stuck in her wheelchair or her short, sharp speech getting louder as she became more exited. On one occasion she apologised because she laughed so much she was sure she wet herself, but it didn't matter because she couldn't feel it anyway!

One day she presented a list to her family and friends and said that she would be very grateful if anyone could help her achieve the following:

- hot-air balloon ride
- racing car ride
- skydive
- marathon
- safari
- swim with dolphins
- see whales
- see the Grand Canyon
- visit San Francisco
- help younger sufferers of MS

Over the years and with the help of her family and friends, Sheena achieved all of these things. Her MS symptoms varied in severity, but she never regained the ability to walk. People continued to be surprised at how she kept on smiling and how she always seemed to choose the positive and optimistic view of life.

'Every person, all the events of your life, are there because you have drawn them there. What you choose to do with them is up to you.'

—Richard Bach

4.   You will be loved.

The chances are that at some point in your life, if not throughout your life, you will be loved. This love may come from your parents, grandparents, brothers, sisters, life partner, friends, spouse, son, or daughter. It certainly won't come from everyone and may even be short lived or poorly expressed, even from those on the previous list. The challenge here is to recognise it, believe it, receive it, and enjoy it!

Some people have real difficulty with this – mainly because they have difficulty loving themselves. They believe that, for some reason, they don't deserve to be loved. This, of course, is irrational, self-critical, negative thinking. Everyone at some point in life, even if it's just at birth, deserves to be loved. It's this lack of receiving love that can become self-fulfilling: not being liked, being lonely, bitter, and twisted, full of anger and hate, and – worse – in trouble with everyone around you, including society in general.

Eventually you convince yourself that you don't deserve to be loved. This cycle must be broken! Learn to receive love, and you will begin to give love, where you will find yourself in good company. Say to yourself, 'I am infinitely valuable, and because I am, so are you!' Begin to recognise the beauty and miracle inside yourself, and you will begin to recognise it in others; they will then recognise it in you.

Jimmy was used to the overzealous and enthusiastic attention of new foster parents. With his fifth set in three years at the age of fourteen, he was becoming a master at getting his own way. This was despite his general demeanour of being sullen, easily agitated, and at times aggressive.

Given half a chance, he would prefer to be in the company of his friends, most of whom were either on ASBOs (Anti-Social Behaviour Order) or in care. Jimmy was badly beaten as a child by his father, despite his mother's feeble, drunken attempts to protect him. Eventually he was left alone, abandoned with only aging grandparents and an auntie in Australia as known relatives.

On one particularly challenging day, Ron and Sue, the foster parents, realised they had a very disturbed teenager on their hands. After repeated requests to turn the music down, they were forced to push open Jimmy's barricaded bedroom door, only to find blood-soaked sheets and a pale-faced, semi-unconscious Jimmy. The doctor at the hospital said that his attempt at suicide was a cry for help so serious that another half-hour delay would have been fatal.

Several months passed, and it was becoming clear to Jimmy that these were very special foster parents. No matter how many times he came in drunk, threw furniture around, or became verbally abusive, the response was the same: calm acceptance of the need for Jimmy to like himself, then love himself in order to stop being angry with the world.

Eventually, through counselling and consistent support, Jimmy was able to forgive his biological parents and begin celebrating that he did have things to offer and that actually he was OK. His self-abuse stopped, he became less sullen and angry, and he stayed with Ron and Sue through his time at college, where he began learning to be a plasterer and joiner. Jimmy stopped blaming everything and everyone else for his past and started his own business, eventually taking on an apprentice who also happened to be a foster child of Ron and Sue. Jimmy was loved and eventually he realised it, which created the capacity for giving a little back.

'The most important thing in life is to learn how to give out love and to let it come in.'

—Morrie Schwartz

5.   You will grieve.

The pain you experience when you lose a loved one is difficult to describe and very personal to each individual. It can be as if your heart has been cut or sliced a thousand times or your insides ripped out, leaving a cold vacuum inside and a sense of total loss and devastation.

The shock of realising or being told of a loved one's death can send us into a rage, denying the news and projecting our anger on those around us. Then comes the feelings of being lost, confused, sad, and – unless checked – depressed, lonely, and isolated.

Most of what I've described is a normal reaction. The first waves of emotion can be over in hours, days, or weeks. The sadness and its development can take months or years. It's important to grieve openly, express the tears and heartache, and try to acknowledge why you are crying. You're crying for yourself; you're crying because of the pain associated with being left behind, of being denied more time, of being denied the experience of growing older together, the regrets of not saying or doing enough, and the acknowledgement and sometimes the fear that you're vulnerable too.

The pain of seeing anyone suffer can also stay with you for a long time. Don't get drawn in and stuck here – it is seductive and can drain the life force out of you. Grieve, and then celebrate the life that was. Think what the person gave you, grow stronger because of it, and carry your loved one's spirit on in your experience and what you choose to do with the rest of your life.

Don't be shy of the dying, and don't wait until your loved ones are dying or dead to tell them you love them. Tell them today!

At the age of fifty-four, I am older than my mother was when she died tragically over thirty years ago of a brain injury following a fall. If my sister was still alive today, she would be forty-four. Alas she died at the age of twenty-five of kidney disease. I still grieve – but not to the extent that the sadness subsumes me nor does it stop me recognising and remembering the precious times I had with my mother and sister.

There can be no pain like it – to experience the life force being sucked from you, leaving a painful vacuum of nothingness that was once the life and presence of a loved one. This inevitable experience is one that cannot be avoided but can be lived through to a healthy outcome. It's important to build in support around you at times of grief and to talk openly about your loss. It's also important to let go and move on and not let the grief hold you back. 'Why,' 'what if,' and 'if only' are trains of thought that can keep you in the shadows of bereavement. Your loved ones would want you to move on and be happy, and you can be stronger and wiser through this experience, acknowledging the gifts they gave you during your time together.

You can always revisit the sadness whenever you chose to – many do during graveside visits and anniversaries – but better to find meaning in your own life and future than to ponder over survivor's guilt and regret for the life that might have been. Celebrate the life that was, and get on with your own.

'Since every death diminishes us a little, we grieve – not so much for the death as for ourselves.'

—Lynn Caine

6.   We are all born good.

That's one thing we all have in common as human beings: we are all born from a mother's womb. At that moment of birth, we are innocent and good. What happens from then onwards will begin to shape and influence our lives. Some are influenced before birth, by the mother's (and father's) choice to jeopardize the health of the unborn child by smoking, drinking, or taking drugs. But mostly we are all given life with the potential to be good in this world.

From birth, we all develop into this rich, diverse human race, dependent upon our genes, our early development experiences, and the choices we make. Essentially, we are all the same in terms of being born human, yet it is incredible how quickly we can dehumanise people – strongly enough to hate or kill them.

Everyone deserves a chance to live a good life. Not everyone gets this. Not everyone is as privileged as you probably are reading this right now. The rich and powerful can sit comfortably and observe; some also judge and belittle in some way, thinking they are better than most.

This is ego (your status, position, role – not the real you) and materialism talking. Often the person's sense of humility is lost, and she/he forgets at one time that she was equal (or close to it, depending on the circumstances of birth) to the person she now judges or criticises.

We may all be born good, but life might not be fair. The good-looking, tall, thin, and rich will have a greater advantage. But no matter. Get over it, and do something about your own position. Realise your full potential.

Give people a chance. Try and create the circumstances where their goodness can thrive. Do not write people off or judge them too soon.

It was the summer of 1959, and a bus drove along the dusty roads of a small town in Mississippi, taking its weary passengers home in the late evening. The driver stopped suddenly – startled by the glare of fire and people carrying flamed torches, shouting and angry. The mob drew closer to the bus, and as soon as its members realised the bus was full of black people, they began banging and beating the sides. The driver managed to manoeuvre away while the passengers, to their horror, saw in the rear view of the bus a black man swinging from a tree, his head stretched to the side as his life jerked to an end through the final kicks of his legs.

Twelve-year-old Marcia was on that bus. She grew up in fear and mistrusted all white folk. Marcia, as an African American, wanted to stop this hate growing inside her and decided to become a nurse. No matter how hard she tried, deep down she felt a difference between how she was in the presence of white folk and in the presence of black folk. The image of the hanged man was still too vivid.

One day whilst she was changing the soiled sheets of an elderly white lady, the lady grabbed her hand and said, 'Forgive me.'

'For what?' Marcia asked.

The lady then burst into tears and disclosed how, as a young woman, she beat the black woman who worked for them because she thought she had stolen some linen sheets. The lady was confused and mistook Marcia for the would-be thief. Marcia calmed her down and eventually reassured her that everything was OK. Reading the patient's file, she discovered that the woman was from the same town that the hanging occurred in. Marcia's fear and resentment returned.

That night Marcia was in a car crash. She was trapped underneath an upturned car and adjacent to a burning vehicle. The paramedic who pulled her out was a young white male who risked his life to save hers. Marcia was not a good patient and discharged herself against medical advice. Her unease about the conflicting love and care she had for her fellow human being and the fear and mistrust she had of white people made it difficult for her to lay, rest and reflect in what was a predominant white working environment.

A few days later she received an arrangement of flowers which was quickly followed by a phone call. Tony, the paramedic who saved her on the night of the accident, invited her to an evening out. The romance that followed blossomed, and eventually after two years of marriage, Marcia's first child was born. That child became a successful entrepreneur and poured back some of his wealth into helping both white and black underprivileged children. Marcia often reflected on how all lives are entwined and that given a chance, despite prejudice and hatred, all people can become loving, accepting, and capable of realising their full potential.

'Birth is the sudden opening of a window, through which you look out upon a stupendous prospect. For what has happened? A miracle. You have exchanged nothing for the possibility of everything.'

—William MacNeile Dixon

7.   Children are for life.

'Look at the beautiful things you can buy for babies these days, sweetheart!'

'It doesn't matter; we are not having a child.'

'Please, please, darling – I always wanted a baby.'

'Do you realise it could cost us over £70,000 – more if we support it through university? Just think what we could do with that money.'

'Yes, but we wouldn't have the love of a child, and you can't buy love!'

'Do you want sleepless nights – not just when they are babies, but also when they are old enough to date, drink, abuse drugs…?!'

'They may not! They may turn into angels.'

'Fat chance! Also, when they are old enough they will fly the nest after years of using us as a cheap hotel. We will probably hardly hear from them, and if we're lucky, we may get a Christmas card.'

'Yes, but we could create a life and give the child a chance.'

'The child may not appreciate the chance. A lot of kids grow up resenting their parents. They end up having a chip on their shoulders for the rest of their lives!'

'No, our children would be very attentive and loving towards us.'

'Our children, now! Whoa – more than one?'

'I think an only child may be lonely – they would be good company for each other.'

'I'm not sure if we can afford it! Do you realise our lives would never be the same again? The dynamics of our children and their lives will always be a concern of ours – watching, caring, hoping, praying. At the same time, letting them go, making mistakes, and us having to listen, support, and be there when they need us – always!'

'Is that a yes, then, sweetheart?'

'Maybe…give me a kiss!'

To a parent, your son and/or daughter will always be your child. A divine right for every child should be to have the choice to be hugged by his or her parent or carer every night in an embrace that says – no matter what – I brought you up in this world, and I will always love you.

Within the slums of Mumbai, children are deliberately disfigured to increase their worth as beggars. In some parts of the world, girls are killed at birth because of the burden of keeping them and their lack of worth as an income generator, or because their parents can't afford a dowry. In Africa and other parts of the world, children starve to death and orphans with Aids are left to die. In certain parts of South America, children live on mountains of rubbish and risk being killed by callous mercenaries as they sleep.

Yet some women are desperate for children and experience years of torment and heartache to give birth. Some will foster and adopt, all in the pursuit of creating that special bond between parent and child. And some will choose not to have children. Yet, children are abused and killed every day. How can this disfigured picture of the way we look after our most vulnerable beings in society coexist?

Children are our future and our legacy. We all have moral obligations to do what we can to ensure that our children experience love and acceptance and that their growth and care are nurtured in such a way that they also learn to pass on that love and care. In doing so, we create a history to be proud of and a future to safeguard us all.

'Making the decision to have a child is momentous. It is to decide forever to have your heart go walking outside your body.'

—Elizabeth Stone

8.   Men love sex; so do women.

What is it about sex? It's one of the biggest, if not *the* biggest, drivers or stimulus for 'business' in the world. Men and women think about it every day. It makes and breaks families; it's risky and potentially fatal, yet is a fundamental and exciting desire for us all. An increasing number of young people are choosing to have sex only as an expression of love and so are waiting for life partners before losing their virginity. Others see sex as just another fun thing to do – no strings attached. Most people are in between – wanting sexual intercourse to be an expression of love or affection in a meaningful relationship. Others say it should just be about making babies!

Whatever the motive, sex is a wonderful opportunity to express intimacy between two people. This is especially true if both people have the freedom to be themselves, giving and receiving and expressing in whatever way is right for them both in order to experience joy and pleasure.

It is amazing how many people develop misunderstandings, nervousness, and inhibitions about the whole area of sexual expression. In doing so, they become trapped in their own fantasies without a channel to release them. They risk becoming socially shy, or they overcompensate by being overtly sexual, sometimes inappropriately. Some just isolate themselves.

It doesn't have to be like this. Get help, talk about it, work through your hang-ups. If you can't talk about it to your partner or friend or family member, then find a counsellor. Having sex is a wonderful, natural form of human expression – a great stress reducer, a great opportunity to really communicate and bring a relationship even closer. It can even potentially bond two people together in an expression of love that lasts eternally. The more comfortable you are with your own sexual self, the more you will enjoy others and the less you will judge others for being different.

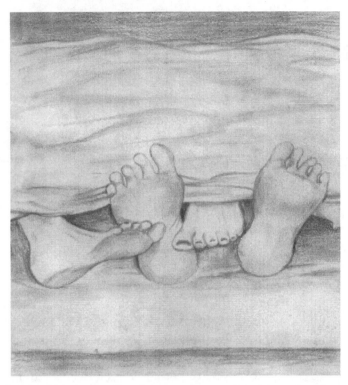

Is it possible to talk about and act freely and enjoy without inhibition and guilt our true sexual nature?

Steve was a shy eighteen-year-old who had been brought up in a strict Methodist environment. At one time he was considering becoming a minister. In his formative years at school, he had a sexual encounter with an older boy that left him confused and excited. His first girlfriend was very stimulating and sexually assertive, but their relationship never went further than heavy petting. He lost his virginity to an older woman who made fun of him, as he was so obviously a virgin.

To Steve sex was fun but confusing. He was unsure of how important it was in the scheme of things and spent his early twenties celebrating his many conquests. It was years before he found the perfect combination of sex and love. His wife was a passionate and loving woman who knew how to give and receive, and Steve learned how to be himself during these passionate embraces.

Now in the vale of his years, he is waiting to rediscover the joy of sex – yet the urgency to do so is less important than the desire to play good golf. Perhaps he still has something to learn about how to freely talk and express his real desires.

'Sex is more than an act of pleasure; it's the ability to feel so close to a person, so connected, so comfortable that it is breathtaking to the point you feel you can't take it! And at that moment, you are part of them.'

—Author unknown

9. Golf and/or a good meal can become more desirable than sex.

There will be a time in your life when the desire to have sex will diminish. You may say to yourself that there are greater pursuits in life, like eating, drinking, hobbies, travelling, and so on. When this happens, you are probably in one of the following categories: you drink too much, you are on medication, you abuse drugs, you have a physical problem, you are having problems in your relationship, you don't communicate very well, you are a person who has taken a vow of chastity, or you're just on your own!

People prefer alternative activities to having sex – or they say they do usually because they're not getting enough! They rationalise it away by making it sound as if somehow they are above it. It may be that illness has caused a loss of libido, or the relationship has become more companionate. It may be that the person is widowed or divorced. Even so, being physical and tender with another person is always a possibility if you wish for it to happen. The tenderness, joy, and excitement that results from the joining of two bodies, even at its most limited embrace, can be experienced regularly as long as we have the breath and physical ability to do so.

When the sexual excitement diminishes from a relationship, it doesn't necessarily mean that the relationship is having problems (it could be, of course), but it might indicate that communication about what each other wants in terms of creativity or enacting a fantasy is missing. One of the advantages of having a stable, trusting relationship is that you can take risks and have fun without the fear of judgement or ridicule. Whether you're eighteen or eighty, these principles apply. So go on – do yourself a favour and have some fun loving each other!

Why compare golf and a good meal with sex when you can have it all? Someone did tell me, however, that a hole-in-one or a meal in one of the top restaurants in the world was as good as an orgasm. Now that I would like to find out for myself!

Steve's closest thing to an orgasm these days is a birdie on the golf course! Does he care? Does it matter? Is it an issue? The answer depends on whether it is an issue with his dear, loving wife, of course. Perhaps the tension and the sense of separateness between them are related. Sex is a form of communication; it can be a communication of love and tenderness, consolidating a love that can sometimes be taken for granted. Whether it becomes an issue for Steve will depend on both his and his wife's willingness to discuss its relevance and importance in their relationship. Of course, having sex – or as some like to refer to it, making love – is not the only way of showing affection and expressing your love.

Embracing, holding hands, a peck on the lips, giving small gifts and messages, knowing that the other person will always be number one when it comes to caring for and supporting each other – these are all important ingredients to a successful, loving relationship. Sex can be either the main event or the sideshow, but it will never replace or be a substitute for the fundamental love that can exist between two people.

'Great food is like great sex. The more you have, the more you want.'

—Gail Greene

10. If energy in is greater than energy out, you will become fat.

The chances are that you, who are reading this right now, are one of the 70 per cent of the Western population who is overweight. (World Health Organisation) It might be that you are the one in four people who are fat or obese! Is it a problem for you?

It is if you are bothered about wanting to live an average lifespan relatively pain free. If you're fat, you will probably die younger and experience some of, if not most of, the following: diabetes, stroke, bowel cancer, high blood pressure, heart disease, arthritis, cataracts, stomach ulcers, leg ulcers –just to name some of the physical problems! If you're obese – i.e., have a waistline over 40 in and/or a Body Mass Index (BMI) over thirty – then you will also have a number of psychological problems. So you choose: do you want to be fat or fit? Only you can sort it.

Conclusive results show that if your waist is bigger than your hips, then you have a three times greater chance of having a heart attack.(The Lancet Medical Journal) This is because of the type of fat laid down around the abdomen, which releases chemicals that interfere with the insulin-release mechanism. This in turn increases the likelihood of overeating and Type 2 diabetes. To calculate your BMI, take your weight (in kilograms) and divide by your height (in metres) squared.

Stop eating for emotional or social reasons; eat only when you're hungry. Ask 'why' when you put food or drink into your mouth. By the way, special diets don't work long term – just eat less and exercise more. Think about the benefits of losing weight: feeling fitter, living longer and free of pain, looking good, increasing your self-esteem, being a better role model for your children, living long enough to see your kids grow up (maybe even see your grandchildren grow up), getting out and about, enjoying activities a lot more – and for a lot longer. Now why would you want to put all that at risk just for a few emotionally satisfying moments of chewing and tasting food?

Come on – what's really important to you? Go for it!

The surgeon's knife cut deeply into the 8-inch layer of fat globular tissue. Peter's wish was to come out of surgery 28 lbs (12.7 kg) lighter. He felt that he deserved this, especially since he had just spent a month dieting to lose 28 lbs (12.7kg) in order to reach the target weight his surgeon required before he would operate. At just over 392 lbs (177 kg), Peter's health was at serious risk, yet years of yo-yoing between binge eating and fad diets resulted in masking and protecting Peter's real identity.

Peter would rather take solace and comfort in eating in front of the TV than face his fear of rejection from others. This fear of rejection was fed by his lack of confidence in relating to others. His poor self-image even before he was obese became a self-fulfilling prophecy and resulted in an actual poor image. Yet the image inside is the defining factor, and Peter had to relearn how to believe in himself again. Peter needed help to believe that he was worthy of love and capable of giving and receiving love. He had to stop using food as an emotional substitute and start treating food as fuel and not as compensation or a crutch in times of stress. He needed to believe his own power of choice and to choose to live and not die. He needed to rediscover the reasons to live longer and healthier, and believe he was capable of achieving an alternative life to the imprisoned version of himself he had so long suffered.

Diets without the desire and belief to be your true self are of very limited worth. Discovering the healthy person you can be is a journey of satisfying surprises and a loving gift to your loved ones.

Peter is now running half marathons!

For further reading on weight loss, see my book *54 Steps to Happiness: How to Lose Weight by Realising What You Want.* *(available at www.54-self-help-books.com)*

'Don't dig your grave with your own knife and fork.'

—English proverb

11. You will make mistakes.

This one is no big deal. In fact, it's a good thing that we do make mistakes, because those moments are great opportunities to learn, grow, and become stronger, giving us confidence to move forward. This, of course, is based on the assumption that you learn from your mistakes.

So you took the wrong direction, you misjudged someone, you said the wrong thing, ticked the wrong box, married the wrong person…with most of these things, you do what you think is right at the time – no one knowingly makes a mistake. Mistakes are usually unconscious incompetence – i.e., you don't know what you don't know.

Learning comes from shifting unconscious incompetence to conscious incompetence. The problem arises when people don't learn from their mistakes, and they repeat the same pattern of behaviour that keeps getting them into trouble. Why do they do this?!

It could be that they're so self-centred, lost in their own fantasy about themselves, that to admit a mistake would mean tainting their image in some way. They would have to develop some humility, which is difficult for the perfect superstars of this world! Or, it could be that they believe that when things go wrong, it's not their fault; it's everybody else's fault. This person has a big blind spot and needs to take personal responsibility a bit more seriously.

Dan and Jes are brother and sister. They were brought up in a middle-class, caring environment and had very happy childhoods that gave them each the ideal start in life. Dan became a successful business person, and Jes spent her life in and out of prison. The main reason why this stark contrast developed in each child's destiny was due to the fact that Dan the entrepreneur learned from his mistakes and Jes the jailbird did not.

Shortly after they passed their driving tests at the age of eighteen, Dan and Jes were both stopped for driving offences. They were banned from driving for twelve months. During this time, Jes was caught again driving recklessly and was banned for a further six months and given a suspended prison sentence.

Dan chose not to drive for another three years, by which time he had matured and could afford to run a small car of his own. Jes got away with the occasional joy ride and stopped driving illegally only after she crashed a 'borrowed' motorbike, narrowly escaping killing herself and her girlfriend.

Both Jes and Dan left school early and drifted from one job to another. Eventually Dan decided to go back to college and gained a basic qualification in business studies. Jes continued to wheel and deal and started buying and selling stolen goods. Jes is currently serving eight years in prison for resisting arrest, causing grievous bodily harm, and possessing and selling crack cocaine. Jes still claims that she had a raw deal in life and that very few of her mistakes were her fault.

'When you make a mistake, don't look back at it too long. Take the reason of the thing into mind and then look forward. Mistakes are lessons of Wisdom. The past cannot be changed. The future is yet in your power.'

—Hugh White

12. You will feel confused, lost, and uncertain.

Confused, lost, and uncertain? Under pressure, don't know which way to turn? Feeling stressed, losing control, recognising this as a critical moment? You are about to make a decision, probably at the worst time. That's because you are unable to see things clearly or weigh things up objectively. Then chill out! Take a deep breath! Buy yourself some time, take the pressure off, take back some control, calm down, and hold off until you're ready.

Firstly, whatever the reason for your confusion or feeling lost – it's a natural reaction. It's a way of telling yourself that you need more time or information, or need more help to understand what's going on. There's nothing wrong with confusion; out of confusion comes insight, new learning – even enlightenment!

What's wrong with being lost? Being lost results in a sense of achievement when you find the right path or a sense of belonging when you are found.

So, whatever the course of your uncertainty, confusion, or sense of loss, transform these feelings to puzzlement, curiosity, and excitement. Take your time; listen to your own heart, sense of judgement, intuition. Look for the coincidences or connections happening around you right now. What's it all saying?

There's a reason why you feel the way you do right now. Learn from it. By the way – there's nothing wrong with embracing the unknown. It can become your friend.

Ged was, as usual, on autopilot driving to work, caught in the slow stream of commuters collectively seeking their places in the machine called 'productivity.' However, this morning was different. As he sat only half listening to the world's depressive news, he glanced to his right and wondered about the actions of the window cleaner he could see on a ladder close by – wondering how simple his job, and probably life, compared to his own. Then a great urge came over him to continue driving and not to stop until he came to the nearest coastal town. This feeling was so strong that Ged seriously started considering what he really wanted. Working long hours and wondering whether his contribution was making a difference combined with a particularly bad period at home – mainly arguing with his wife, particularly about the lack of apparent control he had over his teenage son and wondering all the while where the spark had gone in their relationship.

Ged missed his usual turning to work. He kept going – he knew he couldn't go on like this. He was confused, not sure what to do, but deep down he knew he was unhappy and things had to change. His car phone rang.

'Just to let you know, Ged, Mr Bell has arrived for your nine o'clock meeting.'

'Sorry, Janette, you will have to give him my apologies. I'm not feeling too well, so I won't make it in today.'

'But, Ged, what about this afternoon's conference?'

How could Ged forget this? A chance to present his work to a prestigious audience that had been set up for months.

'I will see how I am feeling later – I will give you a ring.'

'Shall I cancel everything?'

'No, wait, I'll ring you later.'

Ged had to buy some time. He pulled over and got out of the car and took a few deep breaths. As he started to calm down, the cries, screams, and laughter of children playing close by dominated his attention. As he walked around the corner, he came upon the delightful and chaotic sight of very young children playing. It was at that moment he knew things had to change. Ged had lost his sense of fun, his spontaneity, his thirst for playing and for the lighter side of life. His depression was affecting his work and his relationship with his son. He could just run away, take off, and start anew – but he realised this was not the answer and he needed to change.

Ged did go back to work that day; he successfully presented at the conference, and then cleared his diary for the week and planned in quality time with his wife. They had a well overdue and honest appraisal of what was important and what needed to change in order to safeguard their happiness for the future.

'The truth is that our finest moments are most likely to occur when we are feeling deeply uncomfortable, unhappy, or unfulfilled. For it is in such moments, propelled by our discomfort, that we are likely to step out of ruts and start searching for different ways or finer answers.'

— M Scott Peck

13. Organisations or places of work will always demand more than you can give.

Most of us want to do well at work, make the most of our skills and abilities, get some satisfaction from doing a good job, and be recognised and rewarded for doing so. Some call this a work ethic; some call it ambition – or both! Whatever you call it, it can do you in! It's incredible what people do, risk, and give to progress their careers. However, this is only part of it. Seeking recognition and approval from the boss; becoming accepted as a valuable member of the team; gaining status, power, and control; creating a dependency on what you can do; and generating an increasing level of self-importance are all involved in the seductive process of work demanding more than you can give. You begin working longer hours, having breakfast meetings and meetings after work, taking work home at weekends, and even worse, reading work papers before you go to sleep!

You rationalise – saying it's a phase, a busy period, a good investment time. This, of course, is self-deceptive nonsense!

You choose to put work first, believing you will be rewarded. Yes, you will be rewarded – by more work!

You forget you're supposed to be working to live, not living to work. You become so busy that you get trapped in your own ego – the mask of the important person at work who is indispensable. You start saying, 'They need me!'

It's a slippery path because next you start neglecting your family and loved ones, and then wonder why, when you go on holiday, you spend half of it recovering from stress! Eventually, it will make you ill. You could burn out well before you achieve what you're capable of achieving. So ask yourself – why are you working so hard? Have you got the work–life balance you want? Control work: don't let it control you!

The following are real examples, from my consultancy experience, when individuals got their work–life balance wrong.

The national account manager for a large IT company turned up at a hotel to register but couldn't remember why he was there and what he was supposed to be doing or who he was to see. The hotel had to ring his office to get someone to help him, as he was just sitting in the lobby in a daze. Diagnosis: stress/burnout.

The regional manager of a telephone company was frequently leaving his meetings. When he was asked discreetly if he had a problem, he disclosed that he had diarrhoea for the past few weeks. He had not made a connection between stress at work and physical symptoms. Diagnosis: irritable bowel brought on by stress at work.

The organisation development manager casually mentioned to his medical consultant colleague that he had chest pain and thought it was indigestion. He was given an ECG and was admitted straight away. Blood tests confirmed some muscle damage; however, tests indicated no heart attack. Diagnosis: stress at work and home.

Deborah, a senior manager in a retail clothes company, commuted to work most days. This was a two-hour journey each way, on a clear run using the main motorway network. She indicated that it was a good use of her time, as when she was in standing traffic she could either answer and send emails on her BlackBerry or catch up with reading or make telephone calls. She normally left home in the morning between six and half past six and arrived home the same day around half past seven in the evening. Deborah was forced to take time off after a car accident gave her a broken sternum and severe whiplash injuries. Diagnoses: working and driving under stress; poor judgement all round.

It is so easy to get seduced into the importance of the job and the drive to do well and impress. It is important to take time out and ask: What is really important? What am I risking or taking for granted? At the end of the day, what's it all for?

Sometimes it's important to work for that pot of gold. But, other times, it is essential to take time off and to make sure that your most important decisions in the day simply consist of choosing which colour to slide down on the rainbow.'

—Douglas Pagels

14. You will fall in and out of love.

Ah, the joys and pains of falling in and out of love! I'm talking romantic love, the love with your partner, lover, husband, wife, boyfriend, or girlfriend. You will know you are in love, but sometimes people miss the signs of falling *out* of love.

Firstly, being in love is comfortably consuming. Your loved one becomes a natural feature of your daily thinking. In extreme cases, it's a total obsessive thinking, hour by hour, minute by minute. (Be careful not to confuse love with infatuation or lust!)

There is a yearning to be together, an attraction and stimulation when in each other's company, a sense of being whole. You share hopes, fears, dreams; you can communicate in depth and really listen and understand, challenging each other, arguing with a confidence that the outcome will be good because you trust and respect each other.

When you are apart, you want to be together; you share and enjoy things together, plan your future together, laugh and cry together. You passionately care and watch out for each other. It begins to be difficult to imagine life without your loved one. This is a real, mutually supportive partnership, not one based on dependency or control.

Then, something changes. You stop learning about each other. You stop laughing together. You begin to feel a sense of relief when you are apart. You begin to stop showing interest in each other's lives and start to seek separate activities, separate social groups. You stop looking forward to going out together, begin to get bored with each other's company, and begin to pine for the tenderness, the passion, the total care and love you once had! Now, it may be that you are the one-in-a-million couple who finds each other young, has had no other love, and stays with each other for life, a comfortable, lazy river-type of experience. However, most of us are on and off the roller coaster of love. Thrilling, exciting, scary – and it can make you sick! Others avoid the ride completely – scared of getting hurt or remembering being hurt in the past and are sure they don't want it again. Yet the joy and pain of love gives us a depth of richness that is a real celebration of being alive! Embrace, enjoy, love and be loved. Let someone inside, and be close.

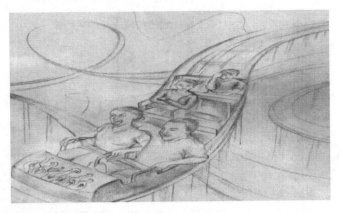

A moment of love

Two flowers in the night
Wake and meet
Petals fall and thrill when
The silkiness of difference enjoy each other's touch

Two flowers in the day
Jointly turn to the sun
Basking in the nourishment and rays of fun
Their buds move closer

Two flowers in the night
Touch and entwine
Their roots mingle
And each other becomes mine

Two flowers in the dawn
Wake and separate
Their bodies stronger and true
Their buds turn and sway to nature's tune
to the music of knowing the joining of beauty

—*Michael Wash, from* 54 Steps to Happiness: How to Lose Weight by Realising What You Want

'Loving is a feeling that brings both joy and pain to my heart. Joy from being with you, being filled with an emotion so deep and tender that no other feeling can compare. Pain from knowing that I'm so in love, that I'm more vulnerable than ever.'

—Author unknown

15. You will become ill.

Our bodies are miraculous, amazing, incredible collections of billions of cells, nerves, blood vessels, muscle – too many different types of tissue to list here, but they are all connected and working 24/7, every second of our lives. It's no wonder that at some point in time, the body will need repairing or healing in some way, due to it becoming out of sorts, injured, or imbalanced. It could be as mild as a cold or as serious as a life-threatening or life-changing disease. Whatever it is, when you are ill, this is the body, your self, telling you – no, shouting at you – that something is wrong. Stop, slow down, pay attention – listen to the wisdom of your body. Pain is there for a reason. Even a discomfort somewhere is saying too much or too little – or I need something else.

Some people ignore their bodies, denying to themselves that anything could be wrong. Frightened because deep down they may have to face the possibility that they could be vulnerable. Ignoring the pain in the stomach, the blood in the urine or stools, the pain in the chest, the dizzy spells, the ringing in the ears, the lump, the swelling, the mole that itches, can have fatal consequences.

Most things wrong with people now can be treated, especially if caught early – so get it checked out! Then ask yourself, 'Why did this happen, why now, is there a reason or a lesson to be learned here?'

Treat not just the body part but the whole self. Use it as an opportunity to review your lifestyle and ask yourself what's really important and what do you have to change in order to get it. You see the world differently when you are ill; sometimes enforced rest, imposed care, and time to reflect can give you new insights into who you are and how you relate to others.

Controlling pain and healing yourself is the greatest challenge – but it can be done. You have to believe you are more than your illness!

I awake with fear and wonderment of hearing my mother's voice as clear as if she was alive today standing next to me. 'Go to the doctor now!' she says firmly.

It was getting bigger and was now uncomfortable; this was not going away. I thought it was an injury following a run, but I knew this swollen testicle was something else. After surgery and still in some considerable pain, I remember the surgeon and his tribe leaning over me and saying, 'Good news – it's not the aggressive type and it's very treatable.'

Some good news – yes – but it was still bloody cancer and I was one testicle down! As far as my wife, sons, and family members were concerned, I was fighting for my life. For me, somehow, deep down I knew I would be OK, but I also knew I would never be the same again.

I am sure they gave me an overdose of radiation on my first treatment; I have never been so sick in all my life. I still get cold sweats today when waiting in an X-ray department. Eight weeks off work was all I could take, but the time off gave my wife and me a lot of thinking time. Our lives were never quite the same again.

'The more serious the illness, the more important it is for you to fight back, mobilising all your resources – spiritual, emotional, intellectual, physical.'

—Norman Cousins

36

16. You will laugh so hard you will cry.

Laughter is great medicine. A laugh a day keeps the doctor away! Why is telling jokes so popular? Why have people made a living out of making people laugh? People like to laugh!

Some are better at it than others, and you will be surprised at what some people laugh at. It's a pure release of emotion, an overt expression of happiness at that moment. Some people are shy or embarrassed at laughing out loud. Don't be! Let it rip – it can be a great stress reducer.

Some people take themselves far too seriously, and we need clowns and comedians to remind us that we are a naturally funny species. When was the last time you looked in the mirror, pulled faces, and laughed at yourself? Never? Then do it! Can't, don't want to? Boy, do you need help taking off that mask of yours. Who are you kidding? Be spontaneous, relax, have some fun – even better, make someone laugh today.

The ultimate overt expression of joy – laughter and tears together – is from the heart. Hold on to those moments, keep them in the memory bank. They may come in handy one day.

'Laughter really could be the best form of medicine' – article by Kate Devlin, *The Telegraph Newspaper,* 16 April 2009

Doctors found that they could potentially cut the risk of people suffering a heart attack by encouraging them to watch comedy programmes. Patients prescribed the 'mirthful laughter' went on to increase the amount of good cholesterol, which protects against heart disease, in their bloodstream. The researchers say that the findings could point to laughter as a useful treatment for a number of conditions.

Dr Lee Berk, from Loma Linda University, California, who led the study, said: 'The best clinicians understand that there is an intrinsic physiological intervention brought about by positive emotions such as mirthful laughter, optimism, and hope.

'Lifestyle choices have a significant impact on health and disease,' he added.

Using laughter as a form of medicine has been suggested for decades; however, there has been little hard evidence of its health effects on patients. For the latest study, patients were asked to select whichever comedy programmes or films that they found the funniest.

They were then asked to watch them for at least half an hour a day over the course of twelve months.

The findings, presented at the Experimental Biology conference in New Orleans, show that after one year the group prescribed laughter saw a 26 per cent rise in their good cholesterol. Patients who took the medication without any extra laughter had just a 3 per cent rise. The group watching comedy programmes also saw a drop of 66 per cent in the amount of harmful C-reactive proteins, which increase the risk of heart disease, in their bodies.

While the control group also saw a fall in the amount of the proteins, it was much smaller at 26 per cent over the course of the year. The study looked at 20 patients with diabetes type 2, a condition which increases the risk of heart problems, who were also suffering from high blood pressure and high cholesterol levels.

The researchers say that the findings show that laughter therapy can also lower stress levels in patients. They called for more research into the use of comedy as a potential treatment for those at risk of developing heart problems.

'I always knew looking back on my tears would bring me laughter, but I never knew looking back on my laughter would make me cry.'

—Cat Stevens

17. You will cry.

When was the last time you had a good cry? Can't remember? Never? Then you are denying yourself a very natural and healthy form of human expression. You're either a man who associates crying with weakness or a source of embarrassment – i.e., 'men don't cry.' Or maybe you've just spent years protecting yourself from being hurt so you keep your feelings to yourself and wonder why you don't have too many close friends or a lifelong partner.

Maybe it's a culture thing, e.g., the British stiff upper lip. Don't cry, be strong – or stop crying, let me hug it better. Whatever is suppressing your feelings is not good for you. It stops you from genuinely exploring your emotions, letting them out, and getting to the real issues. It prevents you from resolving emotional pain. Let it out – cry a little, cry a lot if you have to. If someone starts to cry in your presence, give him or her a tissue – don't hug to make it better (unless the person wants and initiates the hug). Encourage the expression, listen, and try to understand.

Ultimately, crying is associated with some form of physical or emotional pain. Most emotional pain, ultimately, is about loss or fear of loss. Think about it…crying is a release of tension. It's saying 'I have pain, I must express it' – pain associated with the loss of a loved one, loss of freedom, loss of esteem, loss of confidence, loss of friendship. When you cry at something you witness that is sad, such as a film or story, what are the tears about? They are usually about *you*. Celebrate your tears as they can be a path to joy. Don't let pain eat you up inside – let it out!

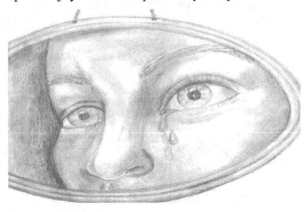

The atmosphere was tense, and we all avoided eye contact. Everyone's eyes were lowered as the facilitator again asked the group to explore our feelings. We all breathed deeply and slowly and were asked to identify our feelings.

We were then asked to explore with a partner what these feelings were. I listened to Cathy as she shared feelings of happiness and gratitude for a wonderful family, then resentment at being taken for granted, then anger for all the things she had not been able to do because she had always put other people first. Her voice was raised, and our facilitator asked her to express more freely her anger. She tried but only with a muted shout, hiding what was probably years of resentment. Her eyes filled with tears and sadness came over her.

We were then asked to change; Cathy asked me to share my feelings. I rambled – excitement, pride, stimulated, happy. Then she asked me to breath, slow down, and be honest with myself. Slowly, I began expressing my sadness, anger, and pain over the loss of my mother and sister. I thought I had come to terms with this – for years I had been carrying the burden of grief, and now I was asked to express this in a group of relative strangers. The facilitator came over, noticing that I was on the edge of something. Then he said the words, 'It's OK – you can cry and be angry at the same time.'

What followed was an intense release of emotion, a flood of uncontrollable tears and a sense of being wronged – of being left without my mother and sister. I curled in a ball and cried for some time. I lost sense of how long it was but became aware of others around me, supporting me. Eventually I came back to the moment. For a while I felt raw and vulnerable – then lightness took over and I could really begin to create space for other feelings now that I had released those emotions pent up inside of me for years. I now value my tears because I realise they are a path to joy.

'Heaven knows we need never be ashamed of our tears, for they are rain upon the blinding dust of earth, overlying our hard hearts.'

—Charles Dickens

18. You will regret some things and feel guilty about some things.

Now, what I am about to ask you to do is not very positive but worth it to make a point. Take a look back over the past. List the things that you have done that you are not proud of, that you regret doing – decisions, mistakes, things you have said or not said, affairs, dishonesty, and so on. Whoops! Still feeling a little guilty? Still getting a few buttons pushed? Starting to think you're not a nice person? *Stop!*

Unless you're a cold, calculating, manipulative psychopath, you will feel at least a little bad about these things. However, it's not worth dwelling on this stuff. Hindsight makes us all wise, and we can spend the rest of our days reflecting on 'if only.' It's important to recognise that these experiences are also part of what makes us who we are today – wiser, older, less likely to do the same again. At the time, we acted out of our own limited awareness. Granted, if we had the power to step back, look forward, and really see the consequences, some of the things we did we might not do – but also, there are many we would still do because it was part of the path leading towards the point we are today – and that's OK! Having a conscience helps you step back and ask yourself what's right at this moment, what are you valuing right now, but it needs to be in the moment – not in the past, where it uses the language of 'should' and 'should not.'

We have to learn to forgive ourselves, move on from the past, live for now, and look forward to the future with renewed optimism. Once we forgive ourselves, we can start to forgive others.

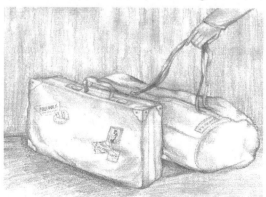

"Father, it is two weeks since my last confession, and I have sinned."

"Tell me, my son, what are your sins?"

"I took 6 pence I found on the kitchen table and spent it on sweets. I ate them all and threatened my sister if she told Mum or Dad I would...."

As a young Catholic boy, I was encouraged to be honest about my wrongdoings. In a way, this was a useful early discipline because it helped me develop a conscience. However, it was so strong and the confessional process so daunting that any wrong act inevitably carried a sentence of long-lasting guilt – even more so if you neglected to confess or tell the full story!

A client of mine named Paul was seeing me for help on a number of issues, but mainly post-traumatic shock and depression following a major road accident in which his son died. Paul was driving. All very understandable; however, this accident happened twenty years ago. The initial problem Paul presented was related to his relationship with his wife – 'we are making each other miserable' – and his fifteen-year-old son, who had started going out and getting drunk. 'I can't control him.' Andrew, his second son, was born five years after the accident.

It had taken Paul three months and six visits before he would start talking openly about the accident. He acknowledged that the undiscussable nature of the event was contributing to a marriage of convenience and superficiality and that his overprotection of his son resulted in Andrew wanting to break free earlier than his father had hoped.

Police reports about the accident indicated no blame attributed to Paul. He and his son were victims of a foreign lorry driver who decided to turn into a dual carriageway the wrong way. The head-on collision killed his son outright, and Paul was in hospital for three months. Paul was still carrying the regret and guilt of 'if only I hadn't insisted on going out that day,' 'if only I was more relaxed about time and set off later,' 'if only I braked earlier or swerved quicker....'

After looking at photos of his dead son, Paul was able to talk directly to him. I then did some joint counselling sessions with his wife. Eventually they started letting go of their guilt and forming a different relationship with each other and their very-much-alive son, Andrew.

Letting Go (author unknown)

To let go is:

Not to cut myself off; it's the realisation that I don't control another.

Not to enable but to allow learning from natural consequences.

To admit powerlessness, which means the outcome is not in my hands.

Not to try to change or blame another; I can only change myself.

Not to care for but to be supportive.

Not to judge but to allow another to be a human being.

Not to be in the middle arranging all the outcomes but to allow others to affect their own outcomes.

Not to be protective; it is to permit another to face reality.

Not to deny but to accept.

Not to nag, scold, or argue but to search out my own shortcomings and to correct them.

Not to adjust everything to my desires but to take each day as it comes and to cherish the moment.

Not to criticise and regulate anyone but to try and become what I dream I can be.

Not to regret the past but to grow and live for the future.

To fear less and love more.

'The beauty of life is, while we cannot undo what is done, we can see it, understand it, learn from it, and change. So that every new moment is spent not in regret, guilt, fear, or anger, but in wisdom, understanding, and love.'

—Jennifer Edwards

19. You will be surprised.

I wake up every morning wondering what the surprise will be today. Life is a wondrous thing, and if you stay alert and awake to what's happening around you, then discovering these surprises will be a delight that will enrich your day and life.

What am I on about? OK, look back on yesterday – at every detail. Did everything happen as it should or as you predicted? Did everything go to plan? I doubt it. Some variation or unexpected event would have happened. What was your reaction? Did you even notice it?

Now, I'm not talking about disasters, accidents, or traumatic events/news. Here I'm referring to the small things – the visitors, the phone calls, the letters, the emails, the insights, the journeys, the places visited and the people we meet and the everyday sights, sounds, tastes, smells, and touches we experience.

If you wake up believing you will be surprised and delighted by these events, then you will. If you wake up dreading these events, then that's likely also. It's called the *self-fulfilling prophecy.* So think positive!! Why would you choose to be negative? For example, if you look close enough at a flower, you will be surprised by its uniform beauty. If you think long enough about someone, you will be surprised how he or she connects to you or contacts you.

Surprise involves you being awake to the connection, the coincidences, and your intuition. It's also about valuing the small things in life, not being so rigid that you discount change or avoid uncertainty. Relax a little, see what's around the corner without a map, and enjoy the surprise of life.

It was the day after Boxing Day, and my wife and I were relaxing in bed with our customary mugs of tea, watching the news. The weather forecast was poor. Snow showers were continuing in the East – right over our heads! However, further west were clear skies but freezing temperatures. Our decision was made: let's go to the Yorkshire Dales – assuming the roads are clear. Why not!? This was the first big surprise of the day: we found a hotel in one of our favourite places. They had a vacancy, so we booked it, packed, and left for a few days of walking in the snow and sun. The following is a description of some surprising and wonderful moments we experienced there:

- walking through ancient woods and seeing the fairy dust sparkle in the sunlight through wispy trees
- looking down on a raging river rolling beneath us and seeing it transform into a winding, meandering, smooth waterway
- feeling the cold air, breathing its freshness, and knowing it was just below freezing – yet feeling warm and nourished inside, the sun on our faces
- slipping on the ice – dicing with danger
- pausing in a field of bulls – feeling intimidated but finding the courage to walk through
- looking above, seeing the white trails of the planes contrasting with the bright blue sky – thinking of all the people travelling to warmer climates
- climbing up steep hills and slippery slopes and squeezing through narrow stiles
- rolling hills and majestic views sparkling in their white majesty
- the comradeship of fellow walkers
- the sound of the birds, the occasional sheep, the rapids of the river, and the crunch of the snow
- the burning hills silhouetted in the dusk sky as the sun dipped in its red glory
- tea and cake in a quaint tea shop in the village

'Surprise is the greatest gift which life can grant us.'
—Boris Pasternak

20. You will experience injustice.

There are many in this world who live with injustice every day. These include those who belong to suppressed religions, political prisoners, those who live in war zones and those who, through no fault of their own, live in families at war with one another.

Living or reacting to injustice can result in outrage and anger, sometimes sufficient to inspire you to demonstrate or take to the streets if the injustice is common to the community. You will feel at some time in your life badly treated – not had a fair hearing, not your fault, something imposed on you with you having little control, often from a more powerful source. What do you do? How do you react? Our initial reaction is often anger and a wish to fight back – whether it's a speeding fine, we're wrongly accused, we're wrongly imprisoned, or we find ourselves on the receiving end of someone else's stupid mistake. It will take courage to fight back, as it is likely you will be fighting forces more powerful than yourself. Before you decide to fight or not, you have to challenge yourself and the circumstances. Is your anger about injustice? Or is it anger with yourself for being in the circumstances to be judged, and are you sure there is no justification?

Once you can stand back and look at the situation rationally – better with friends not as close to the situation to help you – then you have a choice. Some people cope with their anger by fighting the unjust cause for years; others cope by recognising the conviction of their own beliefs, taking comfort in being true to these, and avoiding the circumstances where they were unjustly treated.

The following are extracts from BBC world news Mandela,s life and times. July 2008.

Nelson Mandela, the man credited with ending apartheid in South Africa, marked his ninetieth birthday by calling for the rich to do more for the poor. 'If you are poor, you are not likely to live long,' he said at his village house in Eastern Cape province for a birthday interview.

His predecessor as president, FW de Klerk, described him as one of the greatest figures of the last century.

Mr Mandela was jailed for twenty-seven years for his part in the ANC campaign against white minority rule but went on to become the country's first black president in 1994.

Since stepping down in 1999, he has become South Africa's highest-profile ambassador, campaigning against HIV/Aids and helping to secure his country's right to host the 2010 football World Cup.

In 2004, at the age of eighty-five, Mr Mandela retired from public life to spend more time with his family and friends and engage in 'quiet reflection.'

He appeared before reporters to say, 'There are many people in South Africa who are rich and who can share those riches with those not so fortunate who have not been able to conquer poverty.'

The fight against poverty is one of the causes taken up by Mr Mandela, the BBC's Peter Biles reports from Johannesburg.

Three years ago, the former president attended a huge rally in London as part of the Make Poverty History campaign.

Mr de Klerk, who was awarded the 1993 Nobel Peace Prize along with Mr Mandela, said the former president was a born leader with the 'assurance, the humility, and the grace of a true natural aristocrat.'

As president, he added, Mr Mandela had 'used his personal charm to mould our widely diverse communities into an emerging multicultural nation.' Many of those who have worked with Nelson Mandela and had a close friendship with him over the years say that behind the adulation he inspires there is a very human and often extremely private figure, the BBC's Mike Wooldridge reports.

Fellow Robben Island prisoner Mac Maharaj told our correspondent Mr Mandela was truly an icon. He reduced a veteran white police officer to tears on his inauguration day when he walked over to him, shook his hand, and told him 'today you have become our police.' But Mr Maharaj argues that the event that sheds most light on Nelson Mandela's character was the killing of the popular ANC leader Chris Hani in 1993. Mr Maharaj believes that if Nelson Mandela had called for an insurrection in response it would have been unstoppable but, instead, he went on television to call for calm and commitment to democracy.

'Injustice anywhere is a threat to justice everywhere. We are caught in an inescapable network of mutuality, tied in a single garment of destiny. Whatever affects one directly, affects all indirectly.'

—Martin Luther King Jr

21. You will experience some form of addiction.

Drinking every night? Smoking? Like a gamble? Like to eat and are a bit overweight? Must have your shopping trip? Got to have sex? Hooked into a type of relationship – not necessarily a healthy one?

All these are potentially addictions – they become so when anxiety increases as you think about the possibility of doing without them. Of course, the list doesn't end there, as there are many substances and behaviours that could be addictive.

Why do people become addicted? At a simple level, it's a habit that has gotten out of control – or more accurately, the habit controls the person. At a deeper level, the addiction fulfils some form of gap in life or masks some very real issues. Whatever the reason, it eventually disables the individual and the addiction becomes a life priority – and for some, life itself. It is important to check out those things that you routinely do, habitually do, and ask yourself, 'Is this what I really want? Am I really free to choose not to do these things? Can I choose to stop now?' If the answer is yes, no problem – then challenge again. It could be denial or rationalisation. For example:

- 'I can stop smoking any time, I just don't want to – I enjoy it too much.
- 'I drink a lot – so what? Not as much as many people I know, and anyway, it's good for you.'
- 'I occasionally have a big win. It keeps me going, and who knows – the jackpot could be mine.'

Take the addiction away, and what have you got? Face the real issues, and find the real you!

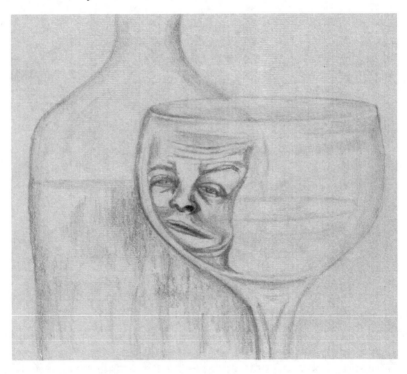

I was escorting Tony for his bath. This was day three on the acute admission ward in a mental health hospital. Tony was in his forties, a large man, amenable and normally cheerful. Today he was shaking, unsteady, and sweating profusely. As I turned off the bath taps, I heard a scream. Turning, I saw Tony leap backwards, hitting his head on the side of the radiator valve so hard that it broke, sending a spurt of hot black water up into the air. Tony was convulsing severely on the floor, blood pouring from his head. I screamed for help!

Stitched up and sedated, Tony spent two days in a side ward. His tranquilisers had been increased, and he seemed to be through the worse. Tony was a dedicated alcoholic – i.e., it was his third admission, always with the claim, 'I mean it this time; I want to give up.'

This claim usually came after a serious delirium tremens reaction (DTs*). Two weeks later, Tony was anticipating the drink challenge. In a perverse way, he was looking forward to it. This would be the only time he would be encouraged to have a drink, under controlled and supervised conditions after being on the drug antabuse. This drug causes a reaction that results in extreme vomiting after the patient drinks alcohol.

After Tony had taken his second pint of beer, he became increasingly red in the face. He took a sip from his third pint of beer and then he erupted, decorating his side ward with sour-smelling, brew-filled vomit. We stood well clear – he wretched for an hour. We cleaned him up. Was that enough? No.

Underlying Tony's addiction was a deep sense of low self-esteem, a failed marriage, a failed business, and an estranged son. What came first, his failures or his addiction? Whatever, Tony chose drink as a solution, which in turn put him on a speedy path to an early and uncomfortable death.

* Delirium Tremens – a severe reaction from the sudden withdrawal of alcohol – symptoms include; sweating, tremors, fits, anxiety and hallucinations.

'I admire addicts. In a world where everybody is waiting for some blithe, random disaster or some sudden disease, the addict has the comfort of knowing what will most likely wait for him down the road. He's taken some control over his ultimate fate, and his addiction keeps the cause of death from being a total surprise.'

—Chuck Palahniuk

22. You will become frightened or fearful.

It's natural to want to protect ourselves from danger. We all want to be safe.

Sometime in your life your safety will be threatened, and you will either freeze with fear, run, or fight. If the situation warrants it, the mind will send messages to and prepare the nerves, muscles, and blood vessels to fight or defend or escape. The adrenalin rushes into action, helping us survive. For some, this reaction can occur just by imagining a fearful situation; that is how phobias develop. Those who want to overcome phobias have to re-educate themselves both at a belief level – i.e., believe the fear is irrational (most spiders don't bite and most planes are safe) – and at a behavioural level – i.e., demonstrate how the body can react differently to these situations.

Getting over a phobia need not be difficult with the right sort of help. The main issue is wanting to, and if the motivation is not there, then you have to ask, 'What is the phobia giving me that I value, or is it been used to disguise the real problem or some insecurity or fear of losing something precious?' Some people enjoy being frightened, hence the popularity of horror films. The thrill seekers taking a risk, putting themselves deliberately in danger, all seems to be related to wanting the 'adrenalin rush' – the shock, almost like a self-test or dare. Does this prove anything? Maybe it is a test of courage. If you want to test your courage and experience those who live with fear and deal with fear on a daily basis, then go and work in the Third World with Aids children or victims of starvation or disaster.

Gandhi once said 'meet your fear and anxiety with an understanding heart and the strength of a powerful warrior, transforming it into a power that can change the world.'

Remember, if your fear is about what might happen, recognise how unreal it is – it's the future; it doesn't exist. It exists only in your mind, and it stops you experiencing what is real now!

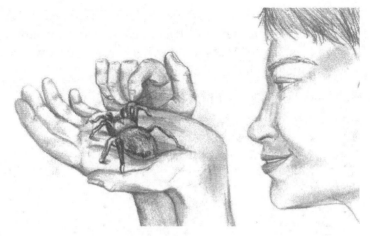

However, being fearful can also be an opportunity to find courage.

INVICTUS

Out of the night that covers me,
Black as the Pit from pole to pole,
I thank whatever gods may be
For my unconquerable soul.

In the fell clutch of circumstance
I have not winced or cried aloud.
Under the bludgeoning of chance
My head is bloody, but unbowed.

Beyond this place of wrath and tears
Looms but the Horror of the shade,
And yet the menace of the years
Finds, and shall find, me unafraid.

It matters not how strait the gate,
How charged with punishments the scroll,
I am the master of my fate:
I am the captain of my soul.

—William Ernest Henley

'Our deepest fear is not that we are inadequate. Our deepest fear is that we are powerful beyond measure. It is our light not our darkness that most frightens us.... As we are liberated from our own fear, our presence automatically liberates others.'

—Nelson Mandela

23. You will become angry.

There will be a time when your blood will boil and you will rage with fury. Or you might just clench your teeth and fists and seethe inside. Or you might be irritated and annoyed with some obnoxious people or situations! Either way, you're angry! In some cases, the anger is hidden deeply – so deeply, the person may come over as the least angry person you know, yet inside, it's eating away and may show itself as an eating disorder, an addiction, or depression.

You have got to deal with anger, or it will deal with you. Anger is a natural reaction to being hurt or the threat of being hurt, injustice, or even the witness to injustice. Something crosses our boundary or challenges our values, takes over control, attacks our freedom – these are things worth standing your corner for and not compromising. Sometimes, however, expressing anger at the time of its cause cannot happen either due to total dominance and fear – for example, in cases of child abuse, recognising the potential of physical danger, personal confrontation. At a less traumatic level, not dealing with the small stuff can lead to a volcanic explosion. In relationships, for example, if you don't deal with the differences as they occur, they will build up until they come out all at once, possibly resulting in a damaging flare-up!

Deal with the small stuff. Don't let it build up; clear the air earlier. Don't seethe inside, or it will make you ill. Find the real issue – deal with it, talk about it. Choose your moments to get angry, and walk away if anger is potentially fuelling aggression and violence. Take it out on a cushion. Shout, rage, cry, and then say to yourself, 'I'm OK. Really, I am.'

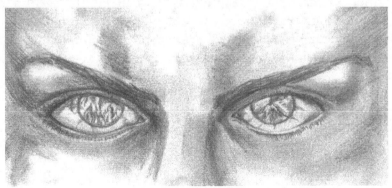

When John sees the 'red mist,' all sense of what is real becomes diverted to vent anger in the most violent way. He has no time to think about the consequences, no time to breathe and stand back, no time to care about anybody or anything other than the urge to spew out an unstoppable burst of lava that destroys anything in its path.

John is serving five years in prison for grievous bodily harm. It could have been worse if his neighbour had not recovered from consciousness. All this over a parking space – or was it?

Everything seemed to be going well for John. He had just been promoted to sales manager in an electrical distribution company. His new home with his wife and infant daughter was taking shape, his older daughter had just started school – yet something was not quite right.

His neighbour seemed fine until one day John was entertaining some friends in his garden, enjoying a barbecue and a few beers. His neighbour leant out of his already open window and shouted, 'I've just put the washing out, you bastard!' then slammed the window shut.

John shrugged it off and put it down to the neighbour having a bad day. After a few weeks in his new home, John noticed that his neighbour and friends were parking their cars in his drive. They had adjoining drives but it was clear whose was whose. Normally this wouldn't bother John, but a few factors were hitting him hard at once. He had thought he had met his quota for sales this month but had just heard a large contract he secured had been cancelled. Since part of his salary was based on commission, this would reduce this month's salary considerably. This month John wanted to pay some of his debt. He liked to gamble on the horses and unfortunately had a bad run and needed to clear his account with his bookie.

After a poor night's sleep due to his daughter being ill and his new baby crying to be fed, John was late for work. Rushing out to his car he discovered his neighbour's car had blocked him in. Still rushing and now fuelled by long-standing irritation, John knocked loudly on his neighbour's door.

His neighbour answered and was confronted with 'Can you move your car off my drive so I can get to work? I'm late as it is!'

'Sure!' the neighbour replied and then shut the door.

John waited for what seemed an age, and then knocked again loudly. The neighbour opened the door again. 'Didn't you hear – I'm late for work. I need you to move your car now!'

'Keep your knickers on, pal – I'll be with you in a minute!'

As the neighbour was about to shut the door, John placed his foot in the way. His neighbour banged John's foot with the door. John pushed the door open and put his hand on his neighbour's shoulder; his neighbour punched John's arm away and the rest was history. John didn't mean to retaliate hard, but unfortunately John's punch caused the neighbour to fall backwards, hitting his head against the radiator and losing consciousness. He was in a coma for three weeks.

If only John had apologised for the barbecue.

If only he had gone round to discuss parking arrangements.

If only he had more control over his gambling and less debt.

If only John managed better the pressure with his new house, new job, new baby.

If only he had phoned into work to say he would be late and bought more time for himself.

If only…

Anger is rarely the result of one single isolated item. It is so often a result of not dealing with many issues, so that eventually they accumulate. And unless the frustrations and pent-up feelings are channelled appropriately, eventually someone will be on the receiving end of that anger and the consequences may be fatal.

'In a controversy, the instant we feel anger, we have already ceased striving for truth and have begun striving for ourselves.'

—Abraham J. Heschel

24. You will feel happy.

It is unlikely you will be happy all of the time, but hopefully, you will find happiness some of the time. Deep happiness can be experienced as pure joy or bliss. This state is rarely experienced and is an illusive goal for even the most dedicated meditator! To be happy is to be content, in tune with all things connected to the flow of life, aware of what's happening within and enabling free choice in everything you do. It can be enhanced by experiencing the beauty in the simple things in life.

Happiness is often associated with success, achievement, clarity of personal direction, and the contributions you make in life. However, it can be fleeting and lost in a moment, as negative experiences pull in the opposite direction and the seduction of material wealth and the power of status feeding the ego take control. Happiness cannot be bought, and often those who have less are happier than those who seem to be wealthy, albeit materially.

Happiness contributes to health and well-being. If you are happy at work, success will come; if you are happy with yourself, love will come. Knowing and accepting who you are is the journey towards peace and happiness.

Ten Keys to Happiness by Deepak Chopra

Physical well-being is inseparable from emotional well-being. Happy people are healthy people. The wisdom traditions of the world tell us that happiness does not depend on what you have, but on who you are. Let's take a moment to reflect on what really creates happiness in us. The following ten keys, gleaned from the wisdom traditions, may give us some insight.

1. Listen to your body's wisdom, which expresses itself through signals of comfort and discomfort. When choosing a certain behaviour, ask your body, 'How do you feel about this?' If your body sends a signal of physical or emotional distress, watch out. If your body sends a signal of comfort and eagerness, proceed.

2. Live in the present, for it is the only moment you have. Keep your attention on what is here and now; look for the fullness in every moment. Accept what comes to you totally and completely so that you can appreciate it, learn from it, and then let it go. The present is as it should be. It reflects infinite laws of Nature that have brought you this exact thought, this exact physical response. This moment is as it is because the universe is as it is. Don't struggle against the infinite scheme of things; instead, be at one with it.

3. Take time to be silent, to meditate, to quiet the internal dialogue. In moments of silence, realise that you are reconnecting to your source of pure awareness. Pay attention to your inner life so that you can be guided by intuition rather than externally imposed interpretations of what is or isn't good for you.

4. Relinquish your need for external approval. You alone are the judge of your worth, and your goal is to discover infinite worth in yourself, no matter what anyone else thinks. There is great freedom in this realisation.

5. When you find yourself reacting with anger or opposition to any person or circumstance, realise that you are only struggling with yourself. Putting up resistance is the response of defences created by old hurts. When you relinquish this anger, you will be healing yourself and cooperating with the flow of the universe.

6. Know that the world 'out there' reflects your reality 'in here.' The people you react to most strongly, whether with love or hate, are projections of your inner world. What you most hate is what you most deny in yourself. What you most love is what you most wish for in yourself. Use the mirror of relationships to guide your evolution. The goal is total self-knowledge. When you achieve that, what you most want will automatically be there, and what you most dislike will disappear.

7. Shed the burden of judgement – you will feel much lighter. Judgement imposes right and wrong on situations that just are. Everything can be understood and forgiven, but when you judge, you cut off understanding and shut down the process of learning to love. In judging others, you reflect your lack of self-acceptance. Remember that every person you forgive adds to your self-love.

8. Don't contaminate your body with toxins, either through food, drink, or toxic emotions. Your body is more than a life-support system. It is the vehicle that will carry you on the journey of your evolution. The health of every cell directly contributes to your state of well-being, because every cell is a point of awareness within the field of awareness that is you.

9. Replace fear-motivated behaviour with love-motivated behaviour. Fear is the product of memory, which dwells in the past. Remembering what hurt us before, we direct our energies towards making certain that an old hurt will not repeat itself. But trying to impose the past on the present will never wipe out the threat of being hurt. That happens only when you find the security of your own being, which is love. Motivated by the truth inside you, you can face any threat because your inner strength is invulnerable to fear.

10. Understand that the physical world is just a mirror of a deeper intelligence. Intelligence is the invisible organiser of all matter and energy, and since a portion of this intelligence resides in you, you share in the organising power of the cosmos. Because you are inseparably linked to everything, you cannot afford to foul the planet's air and water. But at a deeper level,

you cannot afford to live with a toxic mind, because every thought makes an impression on the whole field of intelligence. Living in balance and purity is the highest good for you and the Earth.

Love,
Deepak Chopra

'We tend to forget that happiness doesn't come as a result of getting something we don't have, but rather of recognising and appreciating what we do have.'

—Frederick Keonig

25. You will feel sad.

Feeling sad, down, low, fed up? Then ask yourself, 'Why do I want to feel like this?' What are the benefits of feeling sad? Are you sure you want to continue feeling this way?

If there is a reason, work it out, focus on it. Change it or the circumstances, if you can. If you can't, let it go. It's in the past, it doesn't exist; move on.

Changes in mood happen to us all every day and can be influenced by what we are doing, what we eat, what the weather is like, and who we are with. Some people are energy drainers – they are hard work and permanently suck you dry. Avoid these people! Long winters with little sunshine take their toll; get out and find some sun. Eat fresh food and take exercise. All are good for stimulating the channels in our bodies that lift mood. Look around you; listen to the stories and courage of those who are specially abled and those who have survived disaster, war, or cancer.

Think yourself lucky for what you have, and focus on the positive. The swamps of sadness can trap you – but you can help yourself at this stage. Letting it go further may move you to depression. Now that's when you need professional help!

GUIDELINES FOR CHANGING NEGATIVE TO POSITIVE

(author unknown)

Think well about yourself and your achievements, and take time to reaffirm these on a regular basis. Remember, too, that the basis of being able to love or respect anyone else is to first learn to love and value your own self.

Rather than worry or complain about what you don't have, appreciate what you do have. I believe that there is a basic law in life that says we don't always get what we want, but we get what we need.

Surround yourself with beauty and light, both inside and out.

Do not allow other people's criticism to affect you. Have faith in yourself and your abilities. Remember that criticism is often another way of expressing jealousy and often appears in those who lack self-confidence and self-worth. The unhappy and troubled person can also be critical.

Accept each new circumstance as an opportunity for growth and self-improvement. We learn from experience, whether good or bad.

Every cloud has a silver lining. Even unpleasant events in life have a reason for occurring and come as part of our learning process.

Leave yesterday's sadness behind you and look forward to tomorrow with hope and joy. Why worry over a past event that you cannot change? Let it go.

Don't fret over what is too late to change. Put it down to experience, and remember that yesterday's mistake can be tomorrow's triumph.

Let go of what you no longer need. Even though you may still want it, let the outworn go so that you can be open and receptive to new circumstances.

'You cannot prevent the birds of sadness from passing over your head, but you can prevent them making a nest in your hair.'

—Chinese proverb

26. You will want to win a lot of money.

Have you bought your lottery ticket, entered your football pools, entered the competition with the big prizes, purchased premium bonds? Why? The chances of you winning a life-changing amount is millions to one, yet the amount of money people spend on these and gambling worldwide could wipe out Third-World debt and poverty for millions. Yet we keep doing it, hoping for the dream where money ceases to be a worry. Of course, that's highly unlikely.

Money will be more of a worry, especially if you have more than you need. It's likely to distract you away from what's really important, what you have right now, for example: relationships based on who you are, not based on how much you have. OK, so we would all like enough to pay off our debts; pay the children's debts and set them up in their own homes; buy a new house, new car; travel the world; maybe give a little to charity – yes? Nothing wrong with that – unless, of course, this is your main plan for happiness. Then you have a serious problem!

What are you chasing? Check out how much you really need and for what. Review your lifestyle, slow down and enjoy the bargain of life and the discounts on happiness available today, right now.

Imagine winning the lottery or receiving some other major financial windfall. Initial reactions, no doubt, would be ecstasy, delight, perhaps thinking all your problems were over. Planning would probably have started, in that most people fantasise about winning and talk about what they would do with the money. The usual list of buying a new car, home, having holidays, helping out family members and giving to charity at one level seems apposite. However, beware - there are as many cases of despair following a win, as there are happy ever after endings. Here are a few sad cases;

Poor William 'Bud' Post won $16.2 million in 1988. His brother tried to have him killed for inheritance and his girlfriend tried to sue him. After poor investments he lived his final days surviving on social security payments.

Billie Bob Harrell Jr won $31 million in the Texas lottery in 1977. After 2 years of spending and giving his money away, he committed suicide.

Ken Proxmine only won $1 million. It was enough to move to California and go into business with his brothers. Five years later he was bankrupt and back working hard for a living.

Mark Gardner won the UK National Lottery in 1995 - £11 million. He was very generous helping family and friends with home ownership. However, this led to fall outs, relationship break ups, loss of friendship and family disputes. Fighting depression and anxiety through the support of a psychologist Mark eventually has realised that money cannot buy friendship or love.

Evelyn Adams won the New Jersey lottery twice! The $5.4 million however was not enough to prevent her living in a trailer after years of generosity and gambling.

There are many more tales of woe associated with apparently lucky winners. However, as this simple truth spells out, without love, health, a sense of purpose and an awareness of who you really are, then money can become a dangerous materialistic distraction from what is really important.

'If you have got what you need, you don't need what you want'.

Proverb.

27. You will have a few good friends.

Occasionally, someone will cross your path and you both decide to pause awhile, exchange stories, and then realise that what you are creating between each other is something special. You develop trust, respect, genuine care, and interest in each other – the qualities integral to real friendship. These relationships are often lifelong because the bonds you create through exchanging stories and sharing experiences – plus the value of common interests – can be picked up again anytime, despite years of separation.

You can disclose to a real friend your most intimate fears, knowing that the quality of listening will be supportive and, at the same time, you will get a real, honest answer, which is not always easy to hear. However, some people make the mistake of taking their friends for granted. They make no effort to keep in touch and then wonder why they have so few friends.

Part of friendship is sharing the journey of life, staying in touch and hearing about the ups and downs as life unfolds. A gift of a phone call, a visit, a letter, or an email can be moments enjoyed. Recognise that these types of connections in one's life are rare, so treasure them!

Whilst lying in his hospital bed recovering from the previous day's surgery, Ged heard a familiar cough. Looking up he saw the cheery face of his best friend Patrick. 'OK – cancer, is it? Well, does that mean you are going to die, then?'

Friendship is saying the things many others are frightened to.

Ged eventually tracked down Patrick, who had been missing for days. He knew his friend was in a bad way and had a history of depression. In a small hotel room in a small country village, and despite Patrick insisting that he wanted to be left alone, Ged stayed until Patrick made a commitment and promise to contact Ged if ever he thought about harming himself in any way.

Friendship is being with each other, working through uncomfortable times and always being there in times of need.

Patrick and Ged were struggling to prepare a lesson for their students on the subject of bereavement. They agreed that to teach this subject with integrity, they needed to explore their own grief. Through several hours of tears, they embarked on an emotional journey of sharing each other's stories about their relationships with their mums. The process reconnected them with the pain of their mums both dying relatively young. As a result, they were able to prepare a lesson that their students would be unlikely to forget.

Friendship is the ability to share each other's most painful times, be vulnerable in expressing these moments, and for this process to be OK.

Joan had a few months to live. For years she had worked closely with Patrick and Ged as their secretary and friend. She had been diagnosed as having skin cancer and now, having prepared her husband and two young children, was faced with her ex-bosses insisting that she come out with them.

Joan enjoyed what was to be her last trip out, albeit in a wheelchair. She enjoyed a surreal cup of coffee by the sea, witnessing the sea mist slowly engulf her surrounding in a hazy fog; nevertheless, the moment seemed fitting and significant.

Friendship is facing up to each other's mortality, celebrating the good times and acknowledging endings.

Ged and Patrick were at times inseparable. They produced a training film together, wrote a best-selling textbook and went on holiday together, and enjoyed the occasional overindulgent drink together! Today they live in separate countries, perhaps meeting up once a year and exchanging the occasional email.

Friendship is knowing, despite the distance, that the reunion will be celebratory, emotional, and filled with love.

'Walking with a friend in the dark is better than walking alone in the light.'

—Helen Keller

28. You will mistrust someone.

Not everyone is honourable or has integrity. Some people will try to take advantage of you, and therefore it makes sense, unfortunately, in this day and age, not to be too willing and ready to trust, especially on first meeting or the presentation of superficial credentials.

Mistrust creates suspicion and caution, which can be helpful to distinguish between genuine connections and those that just wish to manipulate you. Once your trust has been broken, it's difficult to regain it as it can affect your confidence and require a leap of faith to forgive and rebuild what was lost.

It's good to leave the door open, but use the safety chain to check out exactly what the contract between you is. Better to make explicit what often is assumed – e.g., confidentiality, standards of behaviour, the importance of repaying a debt and why.

Be careful, however, not to be too mistrusting, as you will likely find yourself always looking for negative aspects of behaviour in others to prove your judgement is right.

Peter was a young man of about twenty-six. He had lived with his parents up until a few months prior to being admitted to an acute male psychiatric ward. He had to be restrained by police after attacking his father and making threats to his neighbours. Peter was diagnosed as having paranoid schizophrenia, in which he perceived everyone and everything in the world with suspicion.

His initial days on the ward were routinely monitored. Clad in an institutional dressing gown and heavily sedated, Peter's world must have seemed like a confused dream state. He would keep his own company, not talk to anyone, and move away from anyone who approached him. I took it upon myself to spend some time just sitting with him initially – bringing him a mug of tea, passing him a newspaper. Then when he was allowed to get dressed, I would walk on the hospital grounds with him. He was compulsorily detained, which means legally he was not allowed to leave the grounds as he was considered to be a danger to himself and others.

One morning as I arrived on duty, I was asked to accompany my colleague to Peter's home address. He had absconded the previous day, and his parents rang the hospital to say he was at home but quite distressed.

Peter's home was an old farm cottage on the outskirts of a small town, about thirty miles from the hospital. Upon arrival we were greeted by two very anxious, elderly parents. Peter had locked himself in his bedroom and was expressing anger and threats to neighbours across the street, whom he thought were directing obscene gestures towards him.

The worrying thing was that Peter's father thought Peter might have a hunting gun with him. We decided to call the local doctor and the police but informed them both to approach discreetly. I thought since I was the one who knew Peter better than most, it might be worth me persuading him to come out of his room and come back with us of his own accord.

I walked up the old narrow staircase and knocked on his door. 'Peter, it's Mike. Can you talk?'

Silence.

'Peter, it's Mike. Remember – from the hospital?'

'I know who you are. Piss off!'

'Your mum and dad are concerned – they want you to come down.'

'Fuck off.'

'We are worried about you. You will get better, but you must let us look after you.'

With that, the door opened. Peter stood facing me. He was a big chap, about my age, and his face was red and his eyes were watering. I noticed that his knuckles, white with rage, were wrapped around a shotgun that he held across his chest.

My stomach churned. I felt sick, and my knees began to shake. 'Peter' I said with a quivering voice.

'Let me pass' he said.

'Come down. Let's have a cup of tea – I'm sure we can sort things out....'

I couldn't believe I was doing this – face-to-face with a paranoid, escaped patient holding a shotgun in his hands.

Peter turned and went back in his room. I sat on the stairs, shaking.

At that moment, the police arrived, followed shortly by the doctor. Reinforcements – I thought I would try once more. 'Peter, come down now with me. Let's chat about it – have a cup of tea and maybe something to eat.'

'I'm not going back to that loony bin!'

'If you don't come down soon and start discussing it, then you will have to be taken back.'

'OK, but promise me I won't go back tonight.'

'I'll see what I can do, but leave the gun in your room.'

Meanwhile, my colleague had briefed the police and the doctor as to the recent events. The police had informed an armed response unit. I was now at the bottom of the stairs as Peter came down gingerly, without the gun. As he entered the room, a police siren deafened the quiet country village. Peter made a run for the front door, and the police jumped, restrained, and handcuffed him. The doctor gave him an intramuscular injection in his backside.

As he lay with his face down, I'll never forget the next moment. He turned his head, stared right at me, and said, 'I trusted you, you bastard!'

Our relationship never recovered from that incident. Even as he improved, he would avoid me. I know I shouldn't take work personally, but this one hurt for a long time.

'You may be deceived if you trust too much, but you will live in torment if you do not trust enough.'

—Frank Crane

29. You will dream.

The brain is the most powerful and least understood organ in the body. It's firing electrical impulses every millisecond of every second of our lives. To function properly, however, it needs sleep to go into quiet mode and recharge. In doing so, deep in our unconscious, the brain still creates images and experiences that are often creative, weird, and free flowing – mainly out of our control.

You may not remember your dreams, but they are there. If you want to recall them, have a pen and paper by your bed and be ready to write down and describe the images you have in your head as you wake up. Dreams are good ways of listening to yourself and using the images to understand what's going on in your life at that moment.

Don't get carried away with other people's interpretations of your dreams. Use your own, and choose a positive interpretation. Here are a few of my own:

- Pressing the accelerator in a car to go faster. It goes into reverse, and I have no brakes – losing control! Meaning: the faster I go, the less progress I make. Slow down!

- Walking in callipers. As I try to run, they snap and break. Meaning: creating more choices in my life – breaking free.

- Falling into a bottomless hole and deliberately free falling to see how deep it is. Meaning: the unknown is not that frightening. Take a risk, and confront my fears.

If you have a nightmare – particularly one you have repeatedly – talk about it, find out what's frightening in reality. Face it and transform it. Some people daydream – this can be OK if fleeting, momentary, or related to hopes and aspirations and then followed up by some action. However, some people daydream to escape reality. This may be a useful survival mechanism, but it can be an excuse for not getting on with life.

Dream away, by all means, but better to turn the dream into a vision and a belief that you can achieve it. Believe in yourself, and others will believe in you too!

Dreams on occasion can guide you to solving a problem or resolving an issue. This happened to me, and it led to a life-and-death decision.

In my early thirties I was quite fit, running most days. One morning I noticed a swelling on one of my testicles. It was after a run, and I put it down to bruising due to a particular pair of ill-fitting pants. I ignored the problem for some weeks; however, I did notice it getting bigger. Having a nursing background with a little knowledge, I put it down to fluid leaking out due to the bruise.

The dream in question involved the one and only time I have ever dreamt about my mother, who died in a tragic accident years ago. It resulted in me listening to her repeatedly saying, 'Look after yourself! Go to the doctor now!'

I woke up that morning holding onto my swollen testicle and knew immediately what to do – still thinking that the visit was being overcautious but knowing it was always important to listen to your mum. Two days after my visit to the doctor, I was admitted to hospital for surgery with a diagnosis of testicular cancer.

'If you can dream it, you can do it.'

—Walt Disney

30. You will become stressed.

Take a moment to think about how you feel right now. Notice your breathing: is it slow and deep or short and shallow? How relaxed do you feel? Do you have a frown on your forehead? Are your shoulders tense? How hard are you holding this book – are your knuckles white? Relax!

Stress can creep up because we get used to carrying it around with us, but eventually, too much stress will do you in. It can cause headaches, sleepless nights, high blood pressure and heart disease, ulcers, even cancer. It can drive you to drink and overeat. All because we get wound up, usually over things we can't do much about anyway!

Have you ever tried navigating through fog when you're lost and driving in dangerous conditions? Ever tried pushing against an immovable object? You can't change the things you have no control over – you can only change yourself. So choose to stop. Stop being stressed, change your circumstances, and put things in perspective. So you think there's never enough time, huh? Rubbish – there is always enough time; it's what you choose to do with it that's important. It's your views about priorities. For example, what's more important – getting to that appointment on time or your health? Why don't you just enjoy the journey? Don't worry about the destination or the time it takes to get there; focus on the moment.

Take yourself out of yourself – look around you, experience more. Why drive yourself so hard? You could probably achieve more by doing less – less with a greater sense of quality, value, and care.

Still don't think you're stressed? You're kidding yourself. Put some relaxing music on, take a bath, or get a massage. Notice the difference before and after. We all need to de-stress from time to time – but most importantly, don't let it build up in the first place. Catch yourself being irritated. Notice the frown, clenched fists, tight shoulders, clenched teeth, and stop. Take a deep breath and ask yourself, 'Is it really worth it?'

Personal Well-Being Checklist
(Adapted from Dr Tim Lowenstein of stressmarket.com)

You can explore the current levels of stress in your life by finding out how many changes you've faced recently. Below is a list of some events that commonly occur in life. Please tick the box if the event has occurred *during the past eighteen months.*

Live Event	Has occurred ✓	Points	Total
Death of a spouse		100	
Divorce		73	
Marital separation		65	
Death of a close family member		63	
Personal injury or illness		53	
Marriage		50	
Significant other fired or made redundant		47	
Marital reconciliation		45	
Retirement		45	
Change in family member's health		44	
Pregnancy		40	
Sex difficulties		39	
Additions to family		39	
Business readjustments		39	

Live Event	Has occurred ✓	Points	Total
Change in financial status		38	
Death of a close friend		37	
Change to different line of work		36	
Change in number of marital arguments		35	
Mortgage or loan for major purchase		31	
Foreclosure of mortgage or loan		30	
Change in work responsibilities		29	
Son or daughter leaving home		29	
Trouble with in-laws		29	
Outstanding personal achievement		28	
Spouse begins or stops work		26	
Starting or finishing school		26	
Change in living conditions		25	
Revision of personal habits		24	
Change in residence		20	
Change in schools		20	
Change in recreational habits		19	
Change in church activities		19	
Change in social activities		18	
Mortgage or loan for lesser purchases (car, TV, and so on)		17	
Change in sleeping habits		16	
Change in number of family gatherings		15	
Change in eating habits		15	
Vacation		13	
Christmas or significant holiday season		12	
Minor violation of law		11	

(Add up the point values applicable to you to obtain your total.)

Total Score:

If you scored 250 or above, then it will be worthwhile to take stock, recognise how stressed you are, and start to work positively towards managing the elements that are causing you stress. Or it's time to do what it takes to recover!

'Stress is basically a disconnection from the earth, a forgetting of the breath. Stress is an ignorant state. It believes that everything is an emergency. Nothing is that important. Just lie down.'

—Natalie Goldberg

'If you are distressed by anything external, the pain is not due to the thing itself, but to your estimate of it; and this you have the power to revoke at any moment.'

—Marcus Aurelius Antonius

31. You will lose something.

Have you had that sinking feeling yet, when you realise you thought you had something, but it's gone missing and you can't recall where you put it nor had it last? That's the moment you experience the value of the possession you have lost. This is small stuff compared with the tragedy of losing one's home through fire or disaster; however, the principles of coping with these situations are the same, albeit varying in degree of severity.

It's easy to get attached to things. We love our cars, our home, our clothes, our watch, and so on. But, at the end of the day, they are just things. Why we get attached to these is because they represent and symbolise emotions, values, and relationships that sometimes are taken for granted in the race to possess more and more.

Stand naked in front of the mirror. Take away all your possessions – what's left? No one can take what remains: a sense of who you really are and how you relate to your loved ones, friends, and colleagues. Don't judge yourself and others on what they own. See through the trappings of material wealth, and value what is genuine, what is real, and what cannot be lost.

It sometimes helps to put things in perspective;

In 2004 over 200,000 people died and nearly 2 million people lost their homes in the tsunami that hit the Indian Ocean and beyond.

In 2005 nearly 2,000 people died and nearly 1 million people lost their homes in Hurricane Katrina that hit the Gulf of Mexico.

In 2005–6 thousands of children died of starvation in the Niger famine.

In 2007 Cyclone Sidr, with winds over 100 miles per hour, killed nearly 3,500 people in southern Bangladesh. The United Nations reported that a million people were without homes (140,000 died in the same area in 1991 due to a cyclone).

In 2008 Cyclone Nargis in the Indian Ocean killed over 130,000 in and around Burma.

In 2009 a 7.6-magnitude earthquake hit the island of Sumatra in Indonesia, leaving more than 1,000 people dead and thousands trapped under the rubble of collapsed buildings in the city of Padang.

In 2010 the Haiti earthquake left between 100,000 and 200,000 dead.

'It is the preoccupation with possessions, more than anything else, that prevents us from living freely and nobly.'

—Henry David Thoreau

32. You will recognise the importance of parenthood. (You will take your parents for granted.)

Most of us grow up with the love and care of parents, a parent, or parent substitutes. When growing up, we know nothing else. Yet when we reach our teenage years, we kick back to discover that we are our own person! Who needs parents? This happens to varying degrees, from aggressive rejection and leaving home, to the occasional temper tantrum.

Moving into adulthood and taking on more responsibility can help heal and re-bond parent/child relationships, especially if acceptance of change is on both sides. However, many children grow away, only to occasionally revisit or call their parents through duty. It's not until they have children of their own that they realise what being a parent means, what a gift of love it actually is.

Some realise too late, when their parents die, and they regret not spending more time with them; gaps in knowledge and appreciation of who they really were occur. Love and cherish your parents. They acted out of love and did the best they could. They still love you.

The Parent's Story

I am are sure it's just a phase! He was such a perfect boy – top in his class, loved sports and music, and he was so polite and spoke so nicely. Where has that gone? I blame the school and the so-called friends he hangs about with. Where on earth did he get the attitude that 'swots are ladging – not cool, Dad!'? Well, thank God he has got the brains – my smart boy. He should be OK and with the right degree will still do well. I mean, he's good at heart. Thank God he's not on drugs or drinking, smoking, or – I can't even think of it – sleeping around. My boy is still my champion, and with the right love and support will come through in the end. I was worried, though, last night when he refused to come home. Should I go and get him and risk alienating him and, worse, embarrassing him in front of his friends? Or should I trust him? Yes, I must trust him. He is a good lad, really, and we love him so dearly.

The Teenager's Story

Why don't they just leave me alone, for God's sake? I'm nearly sixteen! Legally I can have sex (although already done that – no big deal!). They should trust me; it's not as if I'm on drugs or anything – well, not the hard stuff anyway. The occasional spliff and the legal highs, but that's the norm at parties these days. Why don't they just get a life?! I mean, threatening to ground me is so childish – just because I stayed out with my friend. I did phone to tell them. They wanted me to come home – what, at midnight when the party was just getting going? No way! Anyway, if only they knew who I was sleeping with. Now that might tip them over the edge – she's the local barmaid at our pub! So yes, Mum, yes, Dad – I am home. Back to the boring revision, as if I want to go to university. I would leave tomorrow if I could. I know someone who left last year earning a damn site more than those who have just left university. What's the point – can't get a job anyway. God, my parents are so old, so embarrassing, and such a pain. I will be glad when I get a place of my own.

'Romance fails us and so do friendships, but the relationship of parent and child, less noisy than all the others, remains indelible and indestructible, the strongest relationship on earth.'

—Theodor Reik

33. You will be undecided.

There will be a time in your life when you have difficulty making a decision. The difficulty will be because you are either unclear as to the criteria to use or the consequences are too variable, risky, or unknown. Whatever, if you feel under pressure to make a decision when you're not Ready, then buy some time.

There are two major components to decision making: rational or logic, and emotional. In major decisions, it's good to use both. First the logical/rational. Write your lists in columns, side by side. The lists could be cost versus benefits, for and against, short and long term, who is affected for better or worse, risks, right and wrong, and so on. All these could be elements of your lists – negative versus positive. You could even weight (score) each item as to the degree of importance or effect.

Now for the emotional side. Close your eyes, take a deep breath, relax, and imagine you have already made the decision. Do this twice and check out: how does it feel? What does your gut or heart say? Not your head!

Now if the logical method and the heart method are both pointing one way – what's stopping you? If there is a clash…well, for me, I will always go with the heart. For you? Remaining undecided can also be an excuse for staying the same: safe, secure, stable, keeping the status quo – stuck? It's your choice.

A Story of Indecision

When I am on my own – and the decision doesn't involve anyone else – then most of the time it's easy for me to make decisions. What to watch on TV or how long to read, whether to do a bit of gardening or housework, what to eat (although this one can take a little longer, depending on the choice and what phase of dieting I'm in). As soon as my decision involves others, though, oh boy!

What do you think I should do?

What would you rather I do?

How would you feel if I chose this?

I would be happy if we both agreed!

Why don't you choose – I'm happy to go along with what you want!

Familiar? Compromise – I'm good at. Getting what I want – not quite as good.

So, what's that about? Some people say I should assert myself more – but if I do that, I may narrow my choices down in the future by alienating people or coming over as too selfish. Some say I should trust myself more – I do trust myself, but I don't see any problem in considering others when the decision affects more than just me…or am I missing something here?

I am told that the clearer I am about my own sense of purpose, values, and direction, the clearer I can be in my decision making. I also have had the feedback that I can communicate what I want in a way that gives room for others to influence my decision without me compromising too much – this I must learn.

At the end of the day, I need to be true to myself, listen to my head and my heart, and make decisions in my own time. Now, what shall I do with all this insight…?

'Good decisions come from experience; experience comes from bad decisions.'

—Author unknown

34. You will have an accident.

Yes, you will, and you will probably be a major contributor to the accident occurring! Most accidents occur because of a mistake, a lack of care, lack of awareness or concentration, or ignorance or stupidity. It may, of course, be no fault of your own. But it's quite a list to choose from, contributing to accidents that range from a slip of a screwdriver or knife to a fall or a major traffic accident.

When you think you are safe and become complacent about risk, that's when you are most likely to have an accident. When you stop being aware of your circumstances, take for granted your situation, let your mind wander to things other than what you are engaged in – that's when you 'fall.' So when it happens, take it as a warning; it could be worse. You can minimise the amount and degree of severity of accidents by being more sensitive, conscious, aware of yourself and others at all times.

After an accident, ask yourself, 'Why was I in those circumstances in the first place? Could I have prevented it by making different decisions?' In your accident recovery period, take time to re-evaluate. What price or value do you put on your life? Take care of it.

The following list explains the most common contributors to accidents. (Taken from Dobson Associates. Human Performance Consultants)

- *Negligence.* Failure to observe basic safety rules of instructions or failure to maintain equipment.
- *Anger/Temper.* Causes a person to become irrational and disregard common sense.
- *Hasty Decision.* Acting before thinking can lead people to take hazardous shortcuts.
- *Indifference.* A lack of attention to the task – not alert, daydreaming.
- *Distractions.* Interruptions by others, perhaps caused by family troubles, bad news, horseplay while someone performs normal duties or non routine hazardous tasks.
- *Curiosity.* Workers do something unexpected just to see what will happen.
- *Inadequate Instructions.* Results in an untrained or improperly trained worker.
- *Poor Work Habits.* Cluttered floors/work areas, loose clothing, and so on.
- *Overconfidence.* Displayed by behaviour that is too cocky, risky, and macho.
- *Lack of Planning.* Two or more people, each depending on the other to do something, and it doesn't get done.

'On the occasion of every accident that befalls you, remember to turn to yourself and enquire what power you have in turning it to use.'

—Epictetus

35. You will dislike someone.

Wouldn't it be wonderful if we all loved or at least liked each other and lived peacefully? However, there are some people you will just not like – some who no matter how hard you try, you cannot embrace and accept. Why? What's going on? What's the source of your judgement? It is a judgement of sorts. In a way, you're saying, 'This person is less than me, not as good as me. They display behaviours or attitudes I don't like and feel are unacceptable.'

Before you condemn this person, take a look at yourself. Many judgements or criticisms about others are a projection of the same things in ourselves that we deny or can't see for ourselves. For example, our neighbours are always gossiping about us (you're doing the same thing). Why is he so fat? (you struggle to keep your own weight down).

Within each of us are two sides of every aspect of ourselves. Mostly we keep the dark side at bay, but to deny it exists is a risk to one's real self and may end up making you a more bitter, angry, and prejudiced person. Prejudice is a form of dislike or negative judgement based on stereotyping or putting every one of that creed, colour, behaviour, look, and so on into one class. It's a lazy and convenient way of not facing your own fears and misplaced beliefs, and it's an arrogant way of feeling superior. It can lead to hate and war, where prejudice is used to dehumanise others, making it easier to exterminate them.

We all have potential within us to do this. Don't deny it; understand it. The more you can accept the real you, the less you are likely to condemn others for who they are.

Melanie never stops talking about herself and whatever is going on in her world. Oh, she may pause and ask how you are doing, but then after the first sentence she will bring the conversation back to herself, prompting yet another long-winded, detailed account of what happened with her. She seems to be totally self-centred but does try to be liked. However, she does this by abusive humour – that is, she insults people, mocks them, makes sarcastic comments. She thinks it's funny, but actually it can be very hurtful.

Melanie preaches high moral values about being honest, green, community spirited, and family oriented, yet for each of these categories she lives out major discrepancies. She criticises others but is unable to see her own faults!

This description of Melanie is not the most endearing, yet if you listen between the lines and observe what she does, you will find a very generous heart with positive intent. Seeing past initial impressions and recognising that sometimes we judge people on the things we dislike about ourselves can create space to learn more about who people are and allow you to find the part of that person that resonates positively with you.

'Much of our ignorance is ourselves. Our eyes are full of dust. Prejudice blinds us.'

—Abraham Coles

'If we are judging others, we must also be judgemental of ourselves.'

—Lindsey Jackson

36. You will find it difficult to forgive someone.

Someone will hurt you, let you down, or break your trust in him or her. Even worse, you or your loved ones may be violated in some way. An immediate reaction is often anger and the desire for revenge – or at least justice as seen in your eyes. Forgiveness is the last thing on your mind. Some people can never forgive, and the seeds of anger turn to hate and the strains of wanting revenge turn to war. This pattern is passed on from generation to generation, a never ending cycle of bitterness that results always in a lose–lose situation. The only thing that can break this is having the courage to forgive.

By not forgiving, you continue to empower the perpetrator to continue the hurt. This hurt eats inside, creating bitterness, depression, and even disease. To forgive requires stepping outside of the event, recognising the complexity of every situation – e.g., accidental, circumstantial, acting out of limited awareness or ignorance, making a mistake, not realising the consequences of actions, acting out of different beliefs or culture. No one is completely bad; somewhere inside is a good person.

All these are elements or ideas that try to help you rationalise or reason why the event occurred in the first place. On their own, they are not enough. You must also do two more things: look deep in your heart and forgive yourself. Whatever parts you played in the situation – consciously or unconsciously – blaming yourself, feeling guilty, and projecting this on to the perpetrator will block your ability to heal yourself and others.

'If only' is a fantasy in the past that feeds self-blame and negativity. Forgiveness now embraces the moment and gives hope for the future.

Amazing stories of restorative justice can be found on http://www.why-me.org/

Many more resources and stories of inspiration related to forgiveness can be accessed on http://theforgivenessproject.com/

Rwanda has shown the alternative to war through their reconciliation process and the will for the Hutu and Tutsi tribes to live together in peace. This remarkable process, following the genocide of 800,000 Tutsi people within a hundred days in 1994, is a testament to the spirit of humankind and the power of forgiveness. South Africa has also inspired many, in the way they chose forgiveness and reconciliation as a way of recovering from an inhumane apartheid regime.

Without forgiveness, people are in danger of living with bitterness and resentment and continually revisiting the pain associated with the original perpetration. Worse still, the pain may be diverted into revenge, and the cycle of hatred and war is passed from generation to generation. Our only answer to peace within the human race is to find ways to forgive, let go of past atrocities, and talk together to find a way of living with, and respecting our differences. I was inspired to write the following after hearing yet another incident of suicide bombing. The victims' families will find it extremely difficult to forgive and those willing to die for their cause may not realise there is an alternative.

An Appeal to All Those Who Wish to Die for Their Cause

There is a more powerful and effective form of human expression.

It requires greater courage than suicide.

89

The effect lasts longer, and it opens the way to meaningful dialogue.

To some, the thought of it is sickening – breaking through this nauseous barrier can result in sensing a new freedom of the human spirit.

It doesn't require an understanding, appreciation, or acceptance of the other's situation or beliefs – just an acknowledgement that there will always be history and differences. This will not change.

What can change is one's own sense of personal value and the desire for your family and community to live and enjoy the wisdom that comes with growing old together.

Some say, 'It's war!' Yet war is the consequence of any leader's inability to communicate and compromise, with one or both sides assuming a divine right over the other.

Dying for one's cause may seem a glorious act, and some believe it's a way out and into a better life – yet doesn't it mean that no matter how many take this path of glorious suicide, there will always be many more who don't? They will be left behind in treacherous conflict, trapped in a continuous spiral of ever deepening bitterness and sorrow.

Surely there is another way. There is. It's called *forgiveness*.

'We must develop and maintain the capacity to forgive. He who is devoid of the power to forgive is devoid of the power to love.'

—Martin Luther King Jr

37. You will doubt the existence of a God.

Whether you are a strong believer or not, there will be a time when you doubt the existence of a God. Who or what is God will depend on how your religion has encouraged you to express certain beliefs in certain ways. Religious faith can give structure, guidance, and spiritual focus to life's journey.

However, this is not for everyone. Many don't practise religion. This does not mean that they aren't good people or that they are nonbelievers; they may practise their faith in the way they relate to others and how they think about the connections among everything and everyone.

When life seems cruel, demonstrated by a tragic loss of a loved one or a world disaster, then we sometimes hear the phrase, 'How can there be a God who lets this happen?' Or, 'What's the point of praying? God can't make this better.'

Our faith is tested and challenged. Anger at these times is normal. No one will ever prove to you the existence of your God; it is your choice to have faith or not.

Whether you believe or not, many things in life go on unexplained – miracles and faith healing being just a couple. Taking meaning from the scriptures and the stories of holy men and women can teach us wisdom today. We can also find wisdom in quiet, reflective moments, contemplating on who or what is God. So when you doubt the existence of a God, ask yourself, 'What's the point of doubting? I gain nothing. Yet even if I open the door to the possibility, I gain.'

In response to a discussion with my stepdaughter on this topic, I wrote her the following letter.

Will I go to heaven? Is there really a God?

What is this place called heaven? Is it a place or a state of being? I believe it is a state of being – a state that every person searches for, even though some don't know they are searching. The state is total happiness.

To be happy we need to know ourselves deeply to the core and understand who we are in relation to everything else in the world. This is the path of spiritual awareness. Some follow it through institutional religion, some tour the world, others sit under trees and meditate, and some feel the need to preach to others their understanding so they gain comfort in spreading their word.

No one has all the answers.

I believe that Jesus was a healer, a philosopher, and wise man. In his time, the world needed a different way and hence created followers: Christians. The Bible was written by others who were also on the spiritual journey, recording their insights and the events that gave them enlightenment. It's a good book – but so is the Koran.

The messages in the Bible and Christian faith are very similar to all religions: we are all one family; love your neighbour; we are part of everything that goes on in this world, therefore we do care; be non-judgmental and forgive those who trespass upon us.

These and many other core insights into effective and happy living are not easy. They can slip away from us at any time, especially when we are under stress or angry for whatever reason. People take time out to quietly meditate, reflect, and focus on these things almost as a top-up of the 'good stuff' (*faith,* some call it); going to a church or holy site or somewhere full of splendour can have the same effect – for example, the Grand Canyon or the Lakes.

Happiness, and therefore heaven, comes from a deep appreciation of the joy of life and the celebration of what we have. However, there remains a mystery – this thing called God. I believe it refers to the ultimate potential human state, only occasionally discovered through miracles and the unexplained occurrences in life. For example: Indian astrologers writing about your history before you are born; people healing themselves through prayer and positive visualisation; the miracles at Lourdes; telepathy; intuition.

No one knows for definite how the world began. Most recognise the Big Bang explanation – spontaneous explosion of gasses to create a universe – but what else? What was before that? How big is the universe? Is there a power that we do not know having an influence – could this be God?

In a way, it doesn't matter. We are what we are, and we make the most of it. The best is happiness, which cannot be found in material things – only through the love we give and receive.

You have this in abundance! You're one of the most loving people I know, and you are going to make a difference in this world and the next. Ah! – the next?

Yes, I believe there is a next. I believe your spirit never dies. The body does but your spirit lives on. Sometimes it becomes a new person (as evidenced by past lives and reincarnation). Sometimes it disperses into your loved ones, and sometimes both. The spirit of my mum lives in me. My sister, I'm not sure – but I see and sense her a lot, particularly when I feel at risk – so her spirit is protecting me. She said she was going to come back as a magpie, which fits as she was very mischievous!

For children, and to many adults, this thinking is difficult. I believe the institute of the church uses the stories and symbols to get over (for Christians) a Christian way of life, helping people become aware of who they really are and what real happiness is. Then the church leaves it up to individuals to develop how deep they go.

I believe if you are as true to yourself as you can be and do no harm to others, then heaven is an open door. When our bodies die I believe our spirits join with our loved ones, dead and alive, and something special happens; people who die can have more influence on the living than when they were alive. This is through understanding why they were in your life in the first place and what messages they passed on to your own loved ones. This I see from your mum and your nana to you, and this is one reason you have love to pass on to others.

These are great questions to have now, and you will revisit them at different stages in your life. The answers will remain the same, but the meaning will be different.

'Aim at heaven and you will get Earth thrown in. Aim at Earth and you get neither.'

—CS Lewis

38. You will feel misunderstood and not listened to.

Have you ever felt that you're communicating in a vacuum or on another planet? For some reason, even though you think you are speaking the same language, you are just not being heard! So, what do you do? Do you fold your arms, sulk, be quiet, and say to yourself, 'I can't be bothered'? Or do you start arguing or debating or saying something vaguely related to what you're trying to convey?

This is very common, and it involves people following their own agendas and not taking time or making the effort to listen to or understand the other's point of view. If you're the type who sulks and says 'Why doesn't anyone understand me?' then you need to choose whether you want to continue to adopt the 'poor me' script or start to assert yourself a bit more.

Be more open; tell people your wants and intentions. For example: 'I really need you to understand me' or 'Can I have your attention for five minutes?' Give a bit more of yourself, be open and to the point, and be clearer about what you want from a conversation.

Listen more to the other party, and demonstrate the quality of dialogue you enjoy. You are not passive in this process; you can choose to be listened to and understood by creating circumstances where high mutual respect and support are demonstrated through excellent rapport.

For those who want to take the responsibility of listening more effectively, below are some of the training notes I use in programmes to improve listening skills.

Contracting

Appropriate self-introduction and explanation of who and why you are here. Clarify your intentions and the purpose of the conversation.

Ask open questions relevant to what the person is telling you.

Nonverbal Communication

Tone of voice – appropriately soft, warm, and inviting.
Pace – match with the person you are listening to.

Show interest by leaning forward.
Position your self squarely with appropriate space between you.
Be sensitive to cultural differences about the appropriateness of touch

Open/closed – do not slouch or fold your arms.

Eye contact – natural. Avoid staring.
Relax – be genuine/yourself.

Demonstrating Understanding

Paraphrase Repeat back key phrases and words.
Clarify Checking that you have heard correctly.
Be tentative in your response.

Show Empathy

Identify the feelings expressed and check your understanding of the reasons for these feelings.

Summarise

Communicate the key issues and messages in a way that demonstrates you have understood the whole situation.

For those who wish to listen more effectively, you may also have to adopt the following mindset:

- Suspend your judgements until after you have heard the full story.

- Be aware of how your prejudice can colour your listening and influence your understanding.

- Recognise how your own emotional state can determine whether you listen for the positive or the negative.

- Be prepared to give your full attention. Avoid distractions, and concentrate and dedicate all your energy on helping the other tell his or her story. Then follow this up by telling the person what you have heard and understood – without critical judgement.

Listening is a great gift. It is one of the best ways we can demonstrate respect, friendship, and love.

'I know that you believe you understand what you think I said, but I'm not sure you realise that what you heard is not what I meant!'

Robert McCloskey

39. You will want to be on your own sometimes.

How many 'me' moments do you create for yourself in any given day or week – none? Then you are missing a real treat! There will be times when you want to be on your own, because you will need time to think and be yourself, free from distractions. You will want to feel free to express or experience feelings without the inhibition of thinking how others will see you. This can be valuable time away from the strain of life and the demands made upon you. Time to reflect, work things through, or just relax and re-energise.

You don't have to wait for a crisis or the stress levels to peak before you recognise the need for time out. You can plan 'me time' in as a priority – protected time to do exactly what you want, to indulge in whatever works for you. It could be reading, relaxing in a bath with candles, incense, music, or all of this at once; or walking, fishing – whatever! We all need the space to breathe and just 'be.'

If you are seeking out 'me time' more often than not, then you may be quite introverted, shy, or sad. Make sure this is a choice and that you are not avoiding facing your issues. If you're lonely, then seek out company and you will be amazed by how much you have in common with others.

There have been times in my life when I have welcomed being on my own and having my own space – being me – to relax and do my own thing, take time to think in my own time, time to create, time to reflect, time to be. A moment in St Paul's Cathedral on my own resulted in this prayer:

I rest awhile in magnificent splendour,
in touch with unearthly things.
The vastness of my void,
shouts at the future and cries for the past.
My love is immeasurable, my gift unending.
Receive it and live.

As a young man I used to enjoy fishing on my own. It was a time for reflection, as my local river were never abundant with fish – or was it that I was never really much good at it? Either way, I welcomed moments of solitude and found that they resulted in some insightful moments. For example:

Flies, butterflies, and lies,
Bobbing float teasing line.
Thirsty banks holding on
to the variety of man. Time
will tell to gather in the truth.

Life of mine, fishing line.
Catch a moment and live
in the murky river of drought
whose flow stems from heaven
and seeps to the vast ocean of life.

A gasp of air, a painful tug,
The glass edge broken.
The size, a surprise, a child
with trauma, swims back to heal.

The purpose of it all?
All of it purposeful?
Full?
Empty?

There have also been times when I have been lonely: separation from my wife – feeling guilty, unsupported – on my own; working away from home – feeling trapped in hotel rooms in foreign lands; watching rugby on TV – on my own, missing my boys; walking in grief following the funeral of my mother, wanting her by my side.

For me, loneliness is a temporary feeling. I can change it by changing my environment or activity. Solitude is a positive choice for personal space and reflection.

'Language…has created the word *loneliness* to express the pain of being alone. And it has created the word *solitude* to express the glory of being alone.'

—Paul Tillich

40. You will be wrong about things (and right!).

When was the last time you got it really wrong? Made the wrong decision, the wrong judgement, the wrong choice? Rarely, can't remember, or never? Then you, my friend, better check out that ego trip of yours! Arrogance and power have probably gone to your head, and you have created a world of fake wisdom. None of us can be right all of the time – am I right? Who knows? Is there a right and a wrong? It depends on your values, beliefs, culture, moral code – it's hard to tell because there are so many influences.

So why are some people adamant that they're right? We make the best judgement at the time. We choose, we decide with best intentions, taking into consideration all the data or facts available within our limited abilities. So, yes, we are right at the time. But rarely is anything black and white – grey, yes. And it is that grey appreciation that enables people to judge what's right at the time and be open to the possibility that with time, the decision may be wrong. So with humility and tentativeness, they move forward with a willingness to learn and a flexibility to recognise that accommodating others' views can lead to a win–win situation, rather than a win–lose.

The best of us can make mistakes, get it wrong, fall foul of our own judgement at the time. Our saving grace is to accept that we don't have all the answers, we can always learn, and who has ever made it to the top without making mistakes? Being right doesn't always result in the best outcome.

Were Tony Blair and George Bush right to go to war with Iraq? Was America right to go to war with Vietnam? What is right or wrong for Palestine and Israel to try and live together? Is Iran right to build its nuclear capacity? Is China right to suppress access to the Internet?

Is it right to take another's life through capital punishment? Is it right to assist a loved one who wants to die?

Should I be driving a big car? Should I be eating less salt and fat? Should I spend more time on holiday and less at work? Should I say 'I love you' more often? Should I spend more time with my loved ones? Have I got the balance right or wrong?

The Ten Commandments and other spiritual texts are guides and so is the law, but no right or wrong is straightforward; the only true guide is to know deeply what is right and wrong for you – being true to yourself, your loved ones, your values, and your heart.

'If we only talk to people when we are right, we might not achieve as much.'

—George Buchanan

'Anyone who has never made a mistake has never tried anything new.'

—Albert Einstein

41. You will feel underconfident.

What if I get it wrong, make a fool of myself, forget what I'm supposed to be saying? What if they don't like me or I can't get over properly what I'm saying? What if I'm not what they're looking for, if I let them down? What will people think of me? This is all new to me – I don't really know what I'm doing. I just know I'm going to make a mistake!

Any of this sound familiar? Here we have self-doubt, anxiety about performance, and uncertainty about one's own abilities. All normal and understandable; however, if they are not controlled and are allowed to become dominant, they become self-fulfilled –i.e., your fears are realised. So what to do?

Well, first of all, recognise that your main objective is doing yourself justice – not pleasing others; you have no control over other people's reactions to you, so let that one go. Also, go for your own standards that you set for yourself, not ones you imagine others want. You know what you're capable of – go for it on your own terms. Recognise that no one takes on a new job, task, or situation fully competent. Everyone has to learn, and it is this point that's important to convey or realise – i.e., you want to be 'consciously incompetent' so you can identify where and how to improve.

Having a healthy and open attitude to learning will impress more than a slick performance any time. The fact that you are having a go and taking a risk in itself is worthy of celebration. Confidence comes from believing in yourself and knowing that no matter what, you did your best; that makes you a success before you start. So rather than imagining failure, imagine success. See yourself confident, feel calm, think positive – the anxiety will drop enough to allow you to be yourself, which is what most people are looking for.

When feeling underconfident, remind yourself of the following: You have the power to control your thinking and emotions. You can change the way you perceive any situation.

People are often more worried about themselves than you, so focus on them – don't worry about you; this will help you take charge. Ask them about themselves, get them talking, show interest – this breaks the ice and before you know it, the conversation or meeting is easy.

Believe in yourself – no matter what script you have had in the past, no matter how little you have been told about how wonderful you are. You don't need the approval of others; it's nice to have but not necessary. The beauty is within you, so let it shine.

Think positively about any situation; do not dwell on the negative. If you want to use 'what if' thinking, then turn it into 'What if I am successful in this?' Do not put pressure on yourself to be perfect or to be like anyone else; be yourself and celebrate your mistakes because you can learn from them and grow stronger.

When put on the spot, be honest – say what you know, and don't pretend. People prefer genuine and down-to-earth people whose self-esteem is related to knowing who they are, not who they pretend to be through status or fame.

'People are like stained glass windows. They sparkle and shine when the sun is out, but when the darkness sets in, their true beauty is revealed only if there is light from within.'

—Elizabeth Kübler-Ross

42. You will be confronted by change at work.

Face it: organisations have to change or they won't survive. They have to change because of world modernisation and changing consumer expectations. Change may involve a new boss, new systems, a new structure, a new job, a new policy, or a new way of working. Or the organisation may be growing rapidly or be in trouble or about to enter a merger.

Either way, organisations don't change; it's the people in it that do. That means you! The outcome of people changing may mean that the organisation is looking or performing differently, but it has to involve you. So if you feel comfortable in your job, watch out – comfort these days is too temporary.

Look around you – things are changing, and resistance is futile! Better to stay up with what's going on than to be dragged kicking and screaming into the twenty-first century. Resistance, for a while, is rational and can help you buy a little time to come to terms with the inevitable and work out what's really going on. But if you want a healthy and progressive career, you are better to embrace and thrive on change with the intention to learn and improve. For some of you in changing circumstances, if you have the confidence and vision, then leading may be more appropriate than following – i.e., make the change happen in such a way that it becomes welcomed and owned by all concerned.

There are at least 54 ways of managing change at work (see *54 Approaches to Managing Change at Work*, Michael Wash, 3rd Edition, Management Books 2000, published July 2009), and understanding these can give you real insight into how life at work can be meaningful, enjoyable, productive, and life enhancing. Choose where you work and what you do carefully. Are your values in line with your workplace? If not, can you change them to match one another in important areas? If not, you may need to change your job and/or your employer. If work is fun and enjoyable, it ceases to be less like work and becomes more like play.

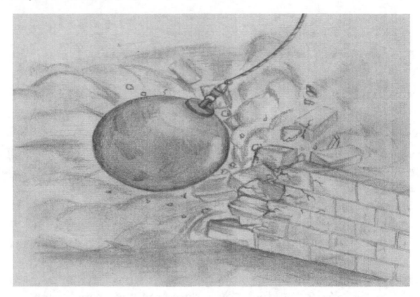

Change begins and is constant throughout my life. Understanding myself throughout change is my desire, yet so hard to do.

To accept my own personal pain as a gift and to recognise my own potential for learning during these times is a challenge, but worthy of celebration.

Letting go of the past and changing myself through the unknown, risks being lost and therefore I can only rely on myself as the guide – this is my hope.

Being conscious in every moment and being aware and responsible for my influence reminds me of my power.

Taking care of myself and being open to receiving creates opportunities for me to give.

I need to learn in order to change; being present and connecting this awareness to my desires for the future will enable me to move.

I can thrive on change and the change of others, for within this learning partnership I can see my worth and the worth of others.

My thirst for knowledge will surround me with books and help me strive for new experiences so I can listen and grow.

I value my tears as I know they are a path to joy.

I strive to listen more to my body so it doesn't have to shout so much.

I pray that what I write becomes real and that I live with a trust that gives me peace.

Michael Wash, from 54 Approaches to Managing Change at Work

'Tell me and I'll forget, show me and I may remember, involve me and I'll understand.'

—Chinese proverb

43. You will seek approval.

Ever been a teacher's pet? What's that about, then? We all like to be liked – don't we? We can experience this desire early on in childhood, where the positive attention, love, and approval of mums and dads are so important to coaching and shaping the learning child. It feels good to be acknowledged and loved; it feels awful to be chastised by someone you respect.

Some people go overboard in the seeking-approval stakes: the 'crawler' or 'sycophant,' the person always sucking up to the boss, the one going over the top to try and win friends over or become the popular centre of attention. This game or approach to trying to get some positive approval / attention is often obvious to everyone but the person playing it. It doesn't work!

Firstly, ask yourself, 'Why do I need this approval in the first place?' This need for external validation is probably driven by either a lack of confidence or esteem, a poor image of self, and uncertainty or belief in who you are. This could be further complicated by your own difficulty in accepting or liking yourself.

It may be that there's a part of you that you're not sure of or you keep feeling guilty about; therefore, it is important to mask this and seek approval from your loved ones or friends about the 'you' they see – but only you can hide that part of yourself that makes you feel ashamed and uncertain. You can cut through all this nonsense by recognising and believing that you are an amazing person; you are OK and loved as you are. There's more chance of you being loved, liked, and accepted by you being yourself – genuine, real, and flawed, as we all are.

No one is perfect, and everyone deserves to be him- or herself! This is, in itself, perfection.

Children need approval to learn right from wrong, positive from negative behaviour. However, they need to develop a healthy sense of self-esteem that becomes less dependent on approval and more about feeling good about themselves. If this is not developed adequately, then children can develop into adults who spend most of their energies trying to please others and become accepted by doing what others do (one of the draws for gang membership) and shying away from expressing what they want. Sometimes to the extent of never knowing what they want or never asserting their needs, thus living by someone else's code. It is important to debunk the negative messages that we pick up from childhood, school, work colleagues, and so on. Let go of criticism, and don't take it to heart. By all means, learn from criticism if it's valid, but remember you are not your behaviour or ability; you are more than this – and that something else is infinitely valuable.

You are beautiful, intelligent, gifted, sensitive, loving, competent, generous, caring, courageous, insightful, dynamic...now add some more and believe it! You have as much right to celebrate you as you as anyone else.

A work colleague of mine once asked, 'What do I need to get your approval?' I replied, 'You will get my approval when you don't need it!'

'About all you can do in life is being who you are. Some people will love you for you. Most will love you for what you can do for them, and some won't like you at all.'

—Rita Mae Brown

44. You will be concerned about what other people think of you.

Does my bum look big in this, darling? Does this tie go with this shirt? How am I seen? What image do I convey? What impact do I want to have? Is it important?

It might be important if you want to create a first impression for a particular job or first meeting. You can spend hours grooming yourself and choosing the 'right' clothes. But at the end of the day, when meeting a person for the first time, his or her judgement will be influenced in the first few seconds by your walk, stance, smile, eye contact, tone of voice, handshake – all wrapped up in whether you are conveying confidence and genuineness.

Of course you may want to fit into a club or certain culture – then yes, you have to be sensitive to how you impact others and decide whether you want to join up or be an outsider. To join up, you conform and become a member.

Some people spend years rebelling against what they see as the norm. They join a fringe group – e.g., tattoos, body piercing, and hairstyles can all be part of the uniform of another group. These groups are trying to find an identity that claims to be different, but it's one that craves for attention. Eventually, most members get tired of creating an image and decide to be themselves.

Most people's judgements or 'what they think of you' are based on very limited awareness or understanding of who you really are. Trying to influence this by conveying a certain image can be a lost cause – superficial and transient, at best. Where it may be important is when someone chooses you to represent them, such as a member of Parliament or staff side (union) representative. Then, the responsibility is yours – to understand how best to represent and demonstrate your understanding, through the way you behave and what you say with integrity, and through your belief that it is right at the time for you and your members.

If your life is dominated by what other people think – if you are an MP, a managing director, a film star, an actor, a top sports personality – then consciousness of and attention to image and how you impress your audience will be crucial. The danger is that many people in these categories will interpret this as 'real life' and forget that the image is a mask, a pretence, a show; it's not the 'real' you. These external impressions can feed the ego, the stakes, the 'perceived' success – but at the end of the day, it's short-lived and takes much energy to keep up appearances.

People need time to be themselves without worrying what others think. Find the real you, enjoy your own company, find self-esteem from within, and don't be dependent on other people's superficial reactions and needy demands. Just enjoy who you really are!

From *54 Steps to Happiness: How to Lose Weight by Realising What You Want by Mike Wash*

How many identities does each of us have? I have the following:

- the business man/executive
- the consultant/trainer
- the husband
- the father, the stepfather
- the gardener
- the actor/singer
- the golfer
- the walker

- the couch potato, TV addict
- the writer
- the Disney fan
- the business-class traveller
- the economy-class traveller
- the brother
- the grandfather
- the nephew
- the uncle
- the drinker, party animal
- the student
- the lover
- the friend
- the grieving son
- the grieving brother
- the dieter
- the fat man
- the rugby union ex-referee/fanatic
- the *Lord of the Rings* and *Star Wars* fan
- the 'not very good' DIY man
- the sentimentalist
- the author
- the dreamer, idealist
- the spiritualist
- the nurse
- the counsellor
- the helper
- the Mercedes driver
- the video/camera man
- the Catholic, the Christian
- the Buddhist

Are these me, or are they roles I play? What is the common thread? Has to be me. I am all these.

'One of the marks of excellent people is that they never compare themselves with others. They only compare themselves with themselves and with past accomplishments and future potential.'

Brian Tracy

45. You will be jealous and envious.

It's a peculiar thing that sometimes, in order to hang on to something; you have to let it go. This is particularly true in relationships because the more you control or try to possess, the more the tension and chances of mistrust and/or jealousy. Jealousy is based on insecurity and mistrust. It develops a belief that one person can have control or a say in what another person does or who the person associates with.

This green-eyed monster will destroy most relationships, and the irony is that it's often based on the jealous person's own personal fears, insecurities, and temptations that they wrestle with in themselves. Being envious of another's situation belongs in the same family of jealousy in that it's a fantasy of what might be, a wish to have something that's not yours, an assumption that the grass is greener on the other side. It's often based on some dissatisfaction or a lack of appreciation of what you have.

Both jealousy and envy take you away from valuing what's real, what's now, what you have. They can be destructive and are a strong signal to tell you to stop and take a long, hard look at yourself and your situation; appreciate what you have. If you are dissatisfied, change yourself and your reaction to the situation or move on. Don't try to control others or try to possess something that's not yours. Make the most of what you have.

Over the years I have on occasion counselled people with relationship problems stemming from a sense of possessiveness, control and mistrust. After one such client session I was inspired to write the following.

Alone with Jealousy

The invasive scent of unwelcome suspicion
takes control, grinding and finding
cause to panic and wonder at what loss
and pain will one's heart prevent
this fragile bond, breaking.

Interrogate or follow.
Observe and search.
Restless till tomorrow.
Continue research
till I find
my peace of mind.

Alas, too late, my search is in vain.
She wanders off despite my pain.
Blind to see what we had,
accusing me as being mad.

I only wanted to hang on to love,
to possess and keep secure
that precious feeling
I thought was ours to endure.

But now I am left
to ponder what is real,
empty and blind.
Wake up inside,
a life to discover –
alone?

'It is in the character of very few men to honour without envy a friend who has prospered.'

—Aeschylus

46. You will trust someone.

Trust is a wonderful thing. It provides confidence and certainty in relationships and agreements. It enables you to let go and relax, believing that what has been contracted will be honoured and respected. Whether it's marriage, fidelity, repayment of a loan, or just being there for a friend, they are all contracts of sorts that bind us together with an expectation of behaving in a certain way.

Sometimes, we take it for granted, especially with our parents, our partners, and even naively so with our children. The reality is that children will have lives they will not want to share fully with their parents; however, parents like to think that their children will do the right thing for health and happiness eventually. When trust goes two ways, it's a positive feeling and creates a sense of freedom that reduces control, judgement, and possessiveness, thus increasing options for a richer experience.

Trust is also about reliance on others to do you no harm and to promote your interests. This enables you to be vulnerable in the presence of those you trust.

A Sister's Trust for Her Brother

Will he get here in time?
Will he be positive and supportive?
Will he be calm?
Will he know what to do if I can't get the pressure right on the kidney dialysis machine?

Will he be able to put the needle in? Will he be gentle?

Will he know what to do if am sick or my blood pressure drops?

Will he stay while I settle and make me laugh?

Will he bring me ice cubes when I want them?

Will he rub my legs when I get cramps?

Will he always be here for me no matter what stupid mistakes I make?

Of course he will!

'When I am trusting and being myself... everything in my life reflects this by falling into place easily, often miraculously.'

—Shakti Gawain

47. You will be generous and selfless.

One of the most selfless and generous acts we can do is to have children. As parents, we give freely of our love and attention, dedicating our lives to ensuring that our children grow up as healthy and as safe as possible. We may even die for them, putting ourselves at risk to save our children, if needed.

We do all this knowing that we will eventually have to let them go so that they can lead their own lives, and we must be prepared to expect nothing in return. We hope, of course, that the bond of love is returned and that eventually our children recognise and value the gift of parenthood.

Other selfless and generous acts may happen when you recognise that you have more than you need. This is more powerful when you see or experience others who have less than they need to survive. Most of the world's population survives on less than $2 a day! This makes you, who are reading this book, very wealthy (assuming you bought it, of course!).

Recognising your privileged position is not enough. You need to have empathy with those less fortunate than yourself. Feeling sorry for others is a wasted emotion; seeing the world from their perspective (empathy) and doing something about it is what's required.

None of us can solve all the world's problems or diminish world poverty, but if we all did something – a little generous and selfless act – then real change would be possible. Try it; you may be surprised! It's amazing how giving freely with no expectation of return creates 'wealth' for you and others.

Gandhi was boarding a train one day with a number of companions and followers, when his shoe fell from his foot and disappeared in the gap between the train and platform. Unable to retrieve it, he took off his other shoe and threw it down by the first. Responding to the puzzlement of his fellow travellers, Gandhi explained that a poor person who finds a single shoe is no better off – what's really helpful is finding a pair.

One night a man came to our house and told me, 'There is a family with eight children. They have not eaten for days.'" I took some food and I went. When I finally came to the family, I saw the faces of those little children disfigured by hunger. There was no sorrow or sadness in their faces, just the deep pain of hunger. I gave the rice to the mother. She divided it in two, and went out, carrying half the rice with her. When she came back, I asked her, 'Where did you go?' She gave me this simple answer, 'To my neighbours – they are hungry also.'

I was not surprised that she gave – because poor people are generous. But I was surprised that she knew they were hungry. As a rule, when we are suffering, we are so focused on ourselves we have no time for others.

—Mother Teresa

Mother Teresa: Love in Action by Niki Collins-Queens (authorsden.com)

In 1952 Mother Teresa began picking up the dying in the streets of Calcutta, India. By the early eighties she and over 3,000 members of her order the Missionaries of Charity were working in fifty-two countries including Europe, the Americas, the Middle East, and Africa and had provided love and comfort to over 42,000 abandoned people in the streets. Paradoxically over half the people recovered. As the Missionaries of Charity flourished and gained attention from the Catholic Church and the world at large, she was considered one of the world's most admired women and in 1979 she was awarded the Nobel Peace Prize.

Now a decade after she died in 1997 at the age eighty-seven, she remains an icon of kindness, love in action, compassion, sacrifice, service, frugality, a transformer of hearts and minds, and a moral example that transcends culture, class and religion.

Her fame did not affect the way she lived. She went barefoot whenever possible and slept on the floor of an open dormitory with the other sisters. She ate lightly, used cold water, owned only two white cotton saris, and washed her own laundry and dishes. Visitors were struck by her simplicity and frugality. She explained, 'No money that is given to the poor should be wasted on our electricity. We use only what we absolutely need.'

She lived Jesus' teaching, 'Whatever you do to the least of my brethren, you do to me.' She saw the poor and the sick as 'Christ in distressing disguise.'

Mother Teresa said, 'At the end of life we will not be judged by how many diplomas we have received, how much money we have made, how many great things we have done.' She believed we will be judged by Jesus' mandate, 'I was hungry and you gave me food, I was naked and you clothed me, I was homeless and you took me in.' She said giving should not only mean satisfying basic needs but being 'hungry for love, naked of human dignity and respect, and homeless because of rejection.' Mother Teresa's goal was not to convert others to Christianity but to allow Hindus to become better Hindus, Christians to become better Christians, and Muslims to become better Muslims. She said, 'We all belong to the same family, Hindus, Muslims and all peoples are our brothers and sisters. They are the children of God.'

The goal of Mother Teresa's worldwide travel and speaking engagements was not to raise funds but to ask her audience to do 'something beautiful for God and serve Jesus in the distressing disguise of the poor.'

The Missionaries of Charity only accepted donations from individuals not corporations. Her vision about money was clear; she asked each person to give until it hurts, not just money but to 'Begin at home by saying good things to your child,' to your spouse, or 'helping someone in need in your community.' As a social critic she replaced indignation with service and said, 'Do what you do with a happy heart.'

When asked about the Catholic Church, woman's roles, or economics she said, 'I don't know about that' or she'd bring the question around to her vision, 'I never look at the masses as my responsibility. I look at the individual...I can only feed one person at a time.... The whole work is only a drop in the ocean. But if I didn't put the drop in, the ocean would be one drop less. Same thing to you, same thing to your family, same thing to your church...just begin...one, one, one.' She said do small things with great love, ordinary things with extraordinary love. 'Love has to be put into action and that action is service.'

'We must give more in order to get more. It is the generous giving of ourselves that produces the generous harvest.'

—Orison Swett Marden

48. You will lie.

It may be a quick reaction to a question that has caught you off guard, and as soon as you respond you may regret it, but too late! You lied and worse – to protect the lie, you have to build a whole web of deceit to create the impression that you are telling the truth!

One reason for lying is to protect an image or perception you think people have of you. This is most common among teenagers to parents: 'No, Dad, I have not been smoking or taking drugs.' 'No, Mum, I haven't slept with him.' 'I never drink and drive.' 'I never look at others or am tempted to be unfaithful.' And so on.

This lying also involves fear of the other's reaction, judgement, and effect on the relationship. Even white lies or fibs – untruths told without intention to seriously or permanently deceive – can result in people questioning your integrity. Most of the time, honesty is the best policy. The only caution here is that sometimes, if the effect of the truth would devastate another and the only reason for telling the truth was to make you feel better and dispel your guilt, then perhaps living with the guilt is preferable. For example a happy marriage where the husband decides to disclose to his wife that he had an affair years ago – to get it off his chest. It serves no purpose other than to hurt his wife. Debate!

Other forms of lying can involve manipulating, controlling, gaining power, or stealing. This can be described as *criminal lying* and unfortunately is not just in the criminal fraternity. It's all around us – in the playground, at home, and at work.

Liars in this category are basically insecure. They have little confidence that they can achieve what they want to achieve without control or manipulation. They can be destructive and unconcerned or unaware of the consequences of their behaviour. Eventually, the vast majority of liars are found out, and unless they change, they become isolated, lonely people – living with superficial, gamey relationships.

Some Well Known Lies

Richard Nixon, the 37th President of the United States, lied and tried to cover up misdeeds in the Watergate scandal.

Bill Clinton, the 42nd President of the United States, denied having sexual relations with Monica Lewinsky.

Was it a lie when Tony Blair, the UK Prime Minister, announced that Iraq had the capacity to launch weapons of mass destruction within 45 mins?

Adolf Hitler, and his generals, published many lies about the Jews to convince the German nation that they were a problem and must be dealt with.

In 1986 Gorbachev denied the seriousness of the problem following the Chernobyl nuclear explosion. The official statement indicated that only 30 people had died and the seriousness of the situation was played down. In fact many thousands had to be evacuated from the area and it is estimated that over 40,000 people have died from the effects of the disaster, mainly cancer related illness.

James Frey's bestselling autobiography was praised and publicised by Oprah Winfrey only to be found out later that much of it was a total fabrication.

Pulitzer Prize winner Janet Cooke won on the basis of a totally fabricated story about a young heroin addict.

Stephen Glass became a successful reporter in the 1990's based on lies, fake websites and sources.

Baron Munchausen is famous for his outlandish stories about his adventures which included going to the moon, riding a cannonball and pulling himself out of a swamp using his own hair. Many children's stories and even a movie is based on his fantasies. There is also a medical condition named after him called the Munchausen syndrome where patients will invent symptoms and illness to get attention.

Other lies we can all relate to include;

The cheque is in the post.
Can you lend me £$xxxx, I will pay you back tomorrow.
It will only take a minute.
Of course you don't look fat in that dress.
I wont be late I promise.
No, I don't smoke, mum.
Sorry I'm late the traffic was dreadful.
Sorry, he is not available right now.
I didn't have that much to drink last night.

'The truth may hurt for a little while, but a lie lasts forever.'

—Author unknown

49. You will be possessive.

Possessiveness in relationships leads to trying to control the uncontrollable and can create jealousy and an unhealthy dynamic between two people. You can't possess a person. No one has a right to dominate, manipulate, or control in a relationship that's based on a contract of partnership – whether this is cohabitation or civil or religious marriage. Possessiveness eventually leads to dependency and mistrust, and the person being dominated loses confidence and eventually self-esteem and becomes trapped. Avoid at all costs – fight for equity, fight to be you.

Protecting what is yours and putting great importance in owning things is another form of possessiveness. This is an understandable aspect of our make-up as humans. Naturally, we are territorial. Unfortunately, this leads to killing one another. Whether it's our home, country, or each other, we will defend at all costs.

Where this natural defensiveness becomes dysfunctional is when it is turned into putting great importance in owning possessions, building your personal wealth, and acquiring bigger and better things in such a way that places other people and yourself lower down on the list of priorities. For example, the senior executive who dedicates his or her life to building a business succeeds, but then is surprised when his or her marriage is on the rocks and the person has high blood pressure, risking heart attack. This is not just about people in high places or powerful positions; it can happen to any of us.

We forget what's important in life; we get carried away with the material excitement of this world. We put great effort into building our homes, extending our gardens, getting the best car, owning and earning more and more.

You can, of course, do all this and be healthy and happy – only if you put health and happiness first!

Eventually Stella turned round to her father and said, 'Dad, I am sixteen. I am no longer your little princess. I can't cope with your interrogation every time I go out. I don't need you to take me everywhere and collect me – you have to trust me more. Please let me go – you are driving me mad. I just feel like running away sometimes!'

Dave's suspicions were right. After following his wife he saw her meet another man. Although they didn't kiss, they seemed close. This was the last straw – how could he keep her? It turned out that the man was her cousin – a quick meeting whilst he was passing through town. However, Dave's challenge started an argument that led to his wife leaving; she felt that after years of mistrust she was being treated as a house pet on a chain!

Andrew couldn't get back home – no flights. The hurricane was still having an effect on all aspect of travel. His last conversation was with his wife who was now in the centre room of the house with their two young children. They had delayed the evacuation warning because one of the children had been out with friends and couldn't be found. Now together they decided to stay. Their last conversation was cut off and all news reports indicated devastation in the area surrounding Andrew's home and family.

Eventually – after twenty-four hours of fear and anxiety thinking the worst – Andrew's heart stopped as he drove down his road. There were very few houses standing. He then recognised one side of his house – his roof had collapsed and there were no signs of life. Fire rescue and ambulance crews were all around. He panicked, ran into the rubble of his home screaming and shouting – and then turned around.

Wrapped in blankets were his wife and two children. 'We have lost everything!' his wife cried.

Andrew replied, 'No, we have what's important and precious. Our family is alive – nothing else matters.'

Rebecca had not slept for days. Anxiety and worry had now developed into irrational fear. She had lost her wedding ring. Stupid, she kept saying, after a diet and recognising her ring needed to be refitted. It must have slipped off somewhere. Was it in the leisure centre? On the golf course? Did she lose it whilst doing the housework? Was it in town when she was shopping?

For days she retraced every step she had taken. She was becoming ill with worry, and her husband was due home from a business trip that evening. How would she tell him? Maybe he wouldn't notice. Maybe she could buy one similar…?

On meeting she told him the harrowing story and it was very obvious to her husband that his dear wife had experienced significant mental torture. That evening he reassured her that the ring would either turn up or something positive would come of it.

A week later, whilst walking in their favourite part of the countryside, her husband paused, held Rebecca's hand, and said, 'Darling, let's renew our vows to each other.'

Tears in her eyes, Rebecca asked, 'How? When?'

He replied, 'Now' and produced a small box. The ring was new – a perfect fit – and their renewal of love for each other was perfect.

'There is nothing wrong with men possessing riches. The wrong comes when the riches possess men.'

Billy Graham

50. You will take for granted your own health and senses.

It's incredible how some people go on day after day, year after year without pausing and considering what they are doing to their bodies. They continue smoking, drinking, and eating to excess, and many take drugs and other abusive, damaging substances. They are slowly destroying what is the most beautiful and sophisticated creation on earth – and why? They believe the short-term high is worth the risk of long-term damage. Ask them again when they are dying of lung or stomach cancer or heart disease. At some point in your life, you will take for granted your health and slip into a lifestyle that neglects the wisdom of the mind and body.

So, if you are mentally stressed, then your body will be stressed too. The mind and body are one – they communicate intimately with each other every second of the day. Your mind can work against you in that it denies or blocks out difficult messages. So, for example, hardened drinkers, smokers, or drug abusers reading this may say to themselves, 'It may happen to some, but it won't necessarily happen to me' – so they give themselves permission to carry on.

Alternatively, they could get 'high' in the beauty and miracle of what they *have*, not what they take in. Imagine not being able to see, hear, touch, smell, or taste. Imagine not being able to walk or talk. Can you?

If you are able to do all these things, then you are very lucky – why put them at risk? Your body and mind need looking after; you need to look after yourself.

Check yourself out and take a healthy, relaxing break to get back in tune with what's really important.

When you light up the next cigarette, think about your loved ones' shock upon hearing the news that you have lung cancer.

When you are recovering from that hangover after a heavy night's drinking, recognise the massive increase in liver disease and lives destroyed due to alcohol abuse.

When you are full but still eating, ask yourself whether you really want to dig your grave with a knife and fork.

When offered the spliff/joint, ecstasy tablet, or other mind-altering substance, ask yourself, 'Why do I want to lose control and live on the edge of a destructive addiction, or worse, risk entering into a drug-induced coma?'

When your feet ache, thank God you have limbs.

When your eyes are tired, thank God you can see.

When you have a cold or the flu, thank God you have some remedy to ease your discomfort.

When you become stressed, thank God you have something to care about.

When you are tired, thank God you have a bed for the night.

When you are hungry, thank God you have the facility to get food.

When you are lost, thank God you have somewhere to go.

We take so much in life for granted. Let's try and keep awake and celebrate what we have before we forget and neglect taking care of ourselves.

'There is no question that the things we think have a tremendous effect upon our bodies. If we can change our thinking, the body frequently heals itself.

—C Everett Koop, MD

51. You will blame someone.

So something goes wrong, who's responsible? Surely someone must take the rap – there has to be someone to blame! Blaming someone for an event or incident happening takes the heat off everyone else. It is a convenient way to focus responsibility onto one or two people, to scapegoat to deflect wider involvement of others. Sometimes it even neglects to deal with why things go wrong, and the issues are never really addressed because the attention is given to the person responsible. The person is dealt with (often punished), but the circumstances that led up to the event in the first place are neglected, and an opportunity to learn and improve is missed.

When you blame someone, you point your finger. When you do, observe the ratio of one finger pointing to that someone and three fingers pointing back to you. The closer you are to an event or issue, the likelier you had a part to play in what happened. Working or living in a blame culture creates an atmosphere of fear and suppresses learning. Mistakes are hidden due to fear of reprisal or humiliation, and eventually, a disaster will occur.

Whose fault is it? Who's to blame? These are poor and ineffective questions. Better to ask: How is it this occurred? What circumstances led to this event? What can we all learn from this? What needs to change?

Blaming others may, for a short while, help us feel superior or good about ourselves. But in effect, we are all part of what goes on in this world, and it takes insightful honesty to recognise this and courage to do something about it!

On 28 January 1986, seven astronauts were killed when the *Challenger* space shuttle exploded shortly after take-off.

Why did the O-rings fail to seal the joint adequately?

Why wasn't the risk assertively communicated and stressed in appropriate language to the launch decision makers?

Why weren't staff members, in particular the engineers, more assertive in communicating their doubts about the safety of the O-ring?

Who decided to launch in low temperature when the risk to the O-ring integrity was high?

Why was NASA experiencing pressure from Congress, the military, and media to launch soon?

Who's to blame?

On 6 March 1987, 197 people drowned because the *Herald of Free Enterprise* ferry capsized shortly after leaving the Belgian port of Zeebrugge.

Why was the person responsible for closing the cargo doors asleep on duty when the ferry left port?

Why did the officer responsible for checking the doors feel under pressure to move on without checking?

Why was the design of the ferry as such that the captain couldn't see the doors from his station?

Why was the ferry on that route when it was inadequately designed for that port?

Who's to blame?

On 6 July 6, 1988, the *Piper Alpha* oil drilling platform exploded, killing 197 men.

Why wouldn't the shift engineer work overtime to ensure that the pressure valve was complete?

Why weren't the permits for pump maintenance and valve replacement coordinated?

Why were the firefighting systems turned to manual?

Why were the firewalls so weak?

Why were the evacuations instructions inadequate?

Why weren't the high-pressure gas pipelines strengthened?

Why didn't the other rigs in the area stop pumping oil?

Why did the rescue rig turn their water pumps on too early, tripping them out, and why was it too slow?

There were only fifty-nine survivors – most of whom survived because they ignored advice and jumped from the burning rig.

Who's to blame?

On 15 April, 1989, 96 football fans died and 766 were injured when the crowds were hurdled into a spaces/pens resulting in a massive crush at Hillsborough Football club, Sheffield.

Why wasn't the start of the game delayed to allow more time for fans to get in?

Why weren't the roadworks on the M62 announced to allow more planning for fans' travel time?

Why were Liverpool fans given the smaller end of the ground when it was predicted they would be the larger crowd?

Why weren't the police better trained to handle crowds, and why did they open gate C?

Why didn't police and stewards redirect fans away from the tunnel entrance?

Why were there inadequate numbers of turnstiles?

Why weren't the pens and fencing removed following previous crushing incidences?

Why did police turn back the ambulances?

Who's to blame?

1,517 lives lost when the Titanic sunk in 1912

The Blame – From the musical *Titanic Lyrics by Maury Yestin*

The scene is set in the ships radio room as realisation that the Titanic is sinking. The owner Bruce Ismay enters and starts accusing Andrews the ships builder and the Captain about their role in contributing to their demise. However Mr Ismay does not seem to be getting away with projecting blame on to his collegues. Bruce Ismay survived, the Captain and Andrews were lost.

CAPT. SMITH
Who called for speed and to break every record!
Who had to keep all the millionaires happy!
ISMAY
How dare you, Smith!
I will not stand here indicted!
Who ignored warnings of icebergs when sighted?
Who, sir, refused to extend up the bulheads?!
ANDREWS
You, sir! To give the first class
Bigger staterooms!
CAPT. SMITH
And who undermined the position of Captain?
ISMAY
And who took a course too far north for the
Season?
CAPT. SMITH
And who kept insisting
We land ever sooner?
ISMAY
And who should have posted
More lookouts in darkness?!
ANDREWS
And who had to have both
The largest and fastest?...
Who did? Who did it? Who did it?

'The best years of your life are the ones in which you decide your problems are yours. You do not blame them on your mother, the ecology, or the president. You realise that you control your own destiny.'

—Albert Ellis

52. You will be faced with a challenge that will consume you and test your resolve to survive.

No one can prepare you for the traumas and tragedies of life. No doubt you will experience the hurt, pain, and devastation associated with your life balance, be it emotional or physical, being threatened. When this happens, it is unlikely that you will be in a fit state of mind to recall what I write here now.

I hope you never experience the following: diagnosis of a terminal illness, your child dies, your parents die young, you become disabled, you are involved in a tragic accident or incident resulting in a loss of function of sorts, other loved ones die tragically, everything around you seems to be falling apart, you file for bankruptcy, you get divorced, you feud with your loved ones – and the list goes on.

It's a depressing list, yet it's reality for the vast majority of people on earth. How do they cope? How can they survive? I am sure there is a point in the traumatic experience where the confidence of survival is low, yet somehow, the resolve of the human spirit breaks through.

You can either choose to be subsumed by events and play the full role of victim, or you can fight for survival. Many people turn the experience around and find deep meaning into why this has happened now, to them. They find a renewed or new purpose and somehow become stronger. As a result of the experience, they are able to help others to either avoid what happened to them or cope better.

Do not underestimate your ability to achieve extraordinary things. Our potential as human beings is phenomenal.

Jane Tomlinson by Martin Wainwright, *The Guardian,* 5 September 2007

Courageous fundraiser who inspired millions with her defiant stand against cancer

Jane Tomlinson, who has died of cancer aged forty-three, seven extraordinary years since she was given six months to live, was an inspirational fundraiser who relished every penny she earned for respite care, nursing, and research into the disease from which she suffered. A cheerful, unassuming everywoman, she was galvanised by her diagnosis to do exceptional things, which raised more than £1.75m. and established a permanent fund that is certain to add plenty more.

Her method was a series of sporting challenges, initially devised with her husband, Mike, and their three children, as a way of making a nonsense of the threat of her aggressive breast cancer. As these feats became more astonishing – in the end including the Ironman triathlon, the world's first marathon run on chemotherapy, and cycle rides across Europe and the US – she developed into a very high-profile campaigner.

This brought controversy, including occasional scepticism that she was not really ill and more considered concern that she might be setting an unrealistic standard for fighting cancer. She responded thoughtfully and without resentment, and seldom, if ever, finished an interview without those present being on her side.

As well as her physical achievements, which have entered the medical literature on staving off terminal disease, she made an important point about the value of relationships to physical well-being. She always began challenges by acknowledging the unwavering support of Mike and the children.

Tomlinson's ordeal began in 1990, when she was the mother of two young girls, living an everyday life in the Leeds suburb of Rothwell. A breast lump proved to be cancer. She had a mastectomy and the lymph nodes under her arms were removed. She then responded to the situation with vigour. She started a three-year radiography course at Leeds teaching hospitals – not as a patient, but as a trainee radiographer. After qualifying in 1993, she took a postgraduate course in specialist radiography for children at Sheffield Hallam University in 1999. All the time, she was a busy mother to two growing daughters, Suzanne and Rebecca, who both won university places, as well as encouraging Mike in his work as an IT consultant.

Meanwhile, however, her cancer had returned and attacked other tissues. Nonetheless, she and Mike went ahead with their third child, Steven, and agreed that they would give the condition a real Yorkshire fight. At the height of her sporting marathons, resting after a cycle leg into Monte Carlo, Jane recalled: 'When I was first told I was going to die, my son was only three, and I could not bear the idea that he would not remember me. At thirty-six, I felt very much that I was too young to die.

'Now, at forty, I feel I have done more than a lot of people do in a lifetime. So if it's my time this year, I would say thank you, God, for what you gave me. I mean, how many other Yorkshire lasses do you know that can say they have cycled to Monte Carlo this afternoon?'

Tomlinson was born in Wakefield, west Yorkshire, the sixth of ten children of a warmly supportive family. Her brother Luke followed her into a medical career and became a senior accident and emergency nurse at St James' University hospital, Leeds. He was also a key part of the family network that encouraged Jane as her sponsored sporting targets increased, cycling with her across Europe in 2004, helping to keep her going at sensible speeds and with prudent rests when the pain increased. Jane and Mike's romance was a local one; they were married in Rothwell, and set up home in the mid-1980s.

The final phase of Jane's life began with her enrolment in a Leeds gym just weeks after her terminal diagnosis in 2000. By May, she was ready to pound round the city's Roundhay Park in a 5 km Race for Life, followed by another 'good cause' event, the 10 km Kirkstall Abbey Dash six months later.

In spite of chemotherapy, the cancer spread to her bones, but she responded with a half-marathon in York and the 2002 London Marathon, which she ran in 4 hrs 53 mins. People started noticing, and she was awarded the title of Yorkshire Woman of Achievement 2002, which tickled her greatly, and chosen to present an honorary baton to the Queen on a visit to Leeds.

Races followed with ever more impressive times – the Great North Run, a cycle ride from Land's End to John O'Groats – alternating with further honours. She was awarded an MBE in 2003, upgraded this summer to a CBE, and honorary degrees. The complications of life in the public eye fazed her comparatively little. Pain and exhaustion led her to twice announce that she was giving up charity spectaculars, but remissions saw her return each time.

Her greatest sporting achievement was the 2004 Ironman, which included a marathon, a 112 mile cycle ride and a 2.4-mile swim, all completed inside seventeen hours. In terms of endurance tests, it was topped last year by her 4,200-mile cycle ride from San Francisco to New York in temperatures topping 100 degrees Fahrenheit on a route which rose above 11,000 ft. When she finally abandoned the marathons last year, Jane put her energies into organising fundraising sports events, via her Jane Appeal – motto: 'Death doesn't arrive with the prognosis.' She leaves Mike, the children, and a grandchild, Suzanne's daughter Emily.

Jane Tomlinson, athlete, charity fundraiser and radiographer, born 21 February 1964; died 3 September 2007.

Copyright Guardian News & Media Ltd 2007.

'Tragedy is a tool for the living to gain wisdom, not a guide by which to live.'

—Robert F. Kennedy

53. We are but a speck in this universe and are connected to everything.

What combines us all as humans? We are all made up of a similar genetic and biological cellular material. We all have our human 'signature' – our DNA – that determines our physiological state. We all live on the same planet in this universe. We are each born from a mother's womb. We all have the basic needs of water, food, warmth, security, and a need to belong with some esteem. All this, only divided by culture, race, politics, and religion – and even in these differences, we will share similar beliefs and aspirations.

We have a lot more in common with our fellow human beings than we sometimes like to recognise. In fact, we are all connected in that whatever we do will, in some way, have a ripple effect and influence others throughout our world.

When we consume or produce, it affects the delicate order or balance on this planet. The more conscious we are of this, the more chance there is of us choosing to be responsible in the way we treat others and the legacy we leave behind us.

Everything on this earth, in this universe, has energy. Everything is consistently vibrating within its own mass of atomic cells, minute specks of energy that give form to their existence. Respecting and using this energy gives us a greater chance of realising how, in the great scheme of things, we are each a mere 'speck' in this universe, yet our presence is so significantly connected to everything else.

Our power and potential is phenomenal. We still have much to learn about being human. There is so much untapped energy, life force, and power. If we could utilise this more at the service of creating a force of goodness, joy, and happiness, then many more opportunities to heal and live in harmony could be created.

Do not underestimate the impact you have on others and your effect on this planet.

'Make time to develop your sensitivity, to respond to 'being' and stop 'doing.' Breathe, reflect, and be humble.'

Lindsey Jackson

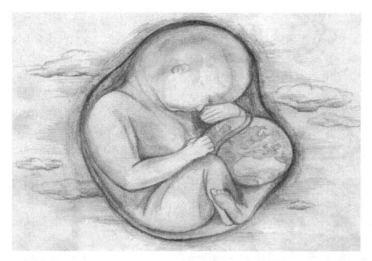

In 1990, the *Voyager 1* space probe sent an image from space looking back at the earth from a distance of around 6 billion km. This photo came to be known as the Pale Blue Dot. In it we can see the Earth as a tiny speck in a vast array of stars and other material. And while it doesn't look like much, the implications of this image are staggering.

Carl Sagan was so moved by this image that he wrote one of the most beautiful pieces on perspective ever written.

Carl Sagan, from *Pale Blue Dot: A Vision of the Human Future in Space,* 1996

Look again at that dot. That's here. That's home. That's us. On it everyone you love, everyone you know, everyone you ever heard of, every human being who ever was, lived out their lives. The aggregate of our joy and suffering, thousands of confident religions, ideologies, and economic doctrines, every hunter and forager, every hero and coward, every creator and destroyer of civilization, every king and peasant, every young couple in love, every mother and father, hopeful child, inventor and explorer, every teacher of morals, every corrupt politician, every 'superstar,' every 'supreme leader,' every saint and sinner in the history of our species lived there – on a mote of dust suspended in a sunbeam.

The Earth is a very small stage in a vast cosmic arena. Think of the rivers of blood spilled by all those generals and emperors so that, in glory and triumph, they could become the momentary masters of a fraction of a dot. Think of the endless cruelties visited by the inhabitants of one corner of this pixel on the scarcely distinguishable inhabitants of some other corner, how frequent their misunderstandings, how eager they are to kill one another, how fervent their hatreds.

Our posturings, our imagined self-importance, the delusion that we have some privileged position in the Universe, are challenged by this point of pale light. Our planet is a lonely speck in the great enveloping cosmic dark. In our obscurity, in all this vastness, there is no hint that help will come from elsewhere to save us from ourselves.

The Earth is the only world known so far to harbor life. There is nowhere else, at least in the near future, to which our species could migrate. Visit, yes. Settle, not yet. Like it or not, for the moment the Earth is where we make our stand.

It has been said that astronomy is a humbling and character-building experience. There is perhaps no better demonstration of the folly of human conceits than this distant image of our tiny world. To me, it underscores our responsibility to deal more kindly with one another, and to preserve and cherish the pale blue dot, the only home we've ever known.

'There are no extra pieces in the Universe. Everyone is here because he or she has a place to fill, and every piece must fit itself into the big jigsaw puzzle.'

—Deepak Chopra

54. The best things in life are free.

What are the best things in life?

Can you beat walking in the fresh air, blue sky, birds singing, experiencing that sensation of awe and humility when you see the beauty of the countryside, mountains, canyons, or waterfalls? Or the sensation on your feet of the sea lapping round your ankles, witnessing the red glory of a sunset as dolphins leap a few feet away from you? Or the tenderness of touch from your loved one? The taste of water on dry lips and throat? The smell of home cooking as you come home from a hard day's work? The ecstasy and thrill of listening to your favourite music?

Each of us has our own list of the best things in life, and most of these will be free. For me, they revolve around the following seven wonders of the world:

1. *Love.* The ultimate expression of acceptance, care, and respect of another person.

2. *Giving.* To truly give without expectation of return and to give back something of yourself within this world.

3. *Receiving.* To accept with graciousness and humility that which comes your way – especially love.

4. *Forgiving.* Recognising that the alternative is a heavy burden to carry, yet forgiveness can free you, and others, to a better life.

5. *Listening.* Listening from the heart and really appreciating what you hear.

6. *Seeing.* Seeing the beauty and miracle in all things.

7. *Touching.* To touch and be touched. Sense the connection, and be in contact with others in this world.

Can you put a price on these wonders? No – embrace and enjoy.

'Life is not measured by the number of breaths we take, but by the moments that take our breath away.'

—Author unknown

And finally...

In reality, life is difficult and very little in life is simple! The truths described here are rarely experienced as simple because we all lead complex, emotional, and interrelated lives. The point about highlighting them as 'simple truths' is to reinforce the importance of our own personal power to chose how we react to situations, make decisions, and form relationships. Fundamentally, we are all striving for the same thing: happiness. I believe within the 'advice' I give related to these truths, the formula for happiness is described. This can be summarised in seven principles:

1. Be genuine, be yourself.
   Know the difference between your ego – i.e., your mask, the image you present to others – and who you really are.

2. Give and receive love.
   Listen and pay real and full attention to those around you.

3. Experience the moment – now!
   The past and future are ideas, thoughts, and imagination. Reality is now!

4. Forgive yourself and forgive others.
   We all act out of our own limited awareness at any given time. We all make mistakes. Let go of grievances, forgive, and you can have peace.

5. Expect surprises – continually learn.
   Nurture your mind. Think positively. Explore the meaning of your coincidences – there is usually a reason why we connect.

6. Eat well and exercise sensibly.
   Take quiet time out to breathe and listen to yourself and your body.

7. Follow your dream, and find your purpose.
   You are infinitely valuable and unique. How do you want to impact this world?

Whatever your quest, your dilemma, your questions, or your hopes and dreams, may your journey be one of integrity with a realised personal choice that gives you fulfilment and happiness.

Other Publications by Michael Wash

54 Approaches to Managing Change at Work

Have you ever wondered why it is so hard to get people to buy in to what seems to be a sensible, or even brilliant, new idea or way of doing things?

Have you ever felt a little uneasy or unsettled when asked to do something new or change something you have been doing for years?

Have you ever wondered why people react in many times strange and obstructive ways to events at work – that should be seen as work?

Have you ever had self-doubt about presenting something that may be new or challenging to your audience?

In this book, I have tried to illustrate the varied approaches (sometime not effective) that people adopt to get others to do things they may initially resist. These approaches also challenge readers to look at themselves and their own willingness to be open to change. The situations cover many work-related (some would say life-related) incidents – e.g., redundancy, stress, imposed new systems, change of job, bullying, promotion and many more. In addition to these examples are exercises to give you feedback on your effectiveness in managing your personal development, time management, meeting effectiveness, and ability to work as a team. A questionnaire on leadership will help you gain insight into your own style of influencing others.

Every manager and supervisor should read this book. If your organisation has courage and wants to create a healthy, thriving work environment, then pass the book on to your staff members and ask them to choose an approach that they would like to discuss!

Good luck dismantling your brick walls!

Available at www.54-self-help-books.com.

54 Tools and Techniques for Business Excellence.

A book of great value to anyone interested in improving his or her personal, team, or organisational business performance.

Simple and practical use with handy hints and tips for success.

Exercises and questions to use with your colleagues.

Techniques tried, tested, and used in the world's best companies.

From the simplest 'generation of ideas' to transforming a total organisation's culture.

DESCRIPTION

The 54 techniques have been used successfully in all types of businesses and organisations, from health service to the airline industry to manufacturing. They form a comprehensive range of techniques for any organisation that is committed to continuous improvement. These are the essential basics: the 'must do' and the 'must know' of management and business excellence.

WHO IS THE BOOK FOR?

Aimed at all managers and staff involved in improvement activities, project management, teamwork, or problem solving.

Valuable aid to trainers and coaches.

Great insight for business students who wish to see theory in action.

Essential for facilitators.

Available at www.54-self-help-books.com.

54 Approaches to Organisational Healing

Reviewers' Comments

The often unhealthy aspects of organisational life are familiar ground; much less familiar are practical approaches to addressing these in a systematic way. This book offers a much-needed helping hand to bring an often daunting challenge down to a workable size for leaders, managers, practitioners, and anyone with an interest in helping organisations work more effectively.

—Graham Barkus, Head of Organisation Development and Learning, Cathay Pacific Airways

This book makes a valuable contribution and is consistent with the values of effective and authentic leadership. The worked examples are extremely helpful, and I wish I had them many years ago. It caused me to reflect, and that's what is really important about any such text – you learn and gain insight.

—Tony Bell OBE, Chief Executive, Liverpool and Broadgreen Hospitals NHS Trust

This book helps managers to identify not just what needs to be done in the moment, but also how open and honest discussion between employees and employers can lead to what Mike Wash describes as 'organisational healing.' Though many of the situations and dialogues are fun to read, they also make the reader squirm with embarrassment from the sheer recollection of having heard these types of conversations before – and yet, done little to bring about learning and renewal in any real or meaningful way.

The 54 approaches illustrate clearly what it takes to sustain health and wealth through the process of work.

—Christopher Bunker, Head of HR Europe, Polaroid Corporation (Part of the Petters Group Worldwide)

Mike Wash developed this approach to organisational healing over a number of years in conjunction with a multitude of clients. Through the pages of this book, he provides a very personal, challenging, and supportive approach into effective ways of constructively challenging the status quo and making difficult issues discussable. The tools and techniques in this book can help you resource a healthy future, improve organisational performance, and establish a very human culture of 'the way we do things around here.'

—George Buchanan, Chief Executive (retired) various Health Service Trusts

Mike Wash uses his vast experience of people, organisations, and processes to enable readers to enhance themselves, their organisations, and their lives. This book will be invaluable for CEOs, MDs, coaches, and anyone working, needing, or choosing to heal their organisation. I shall recommend this to all my students as absolutely essential reading.

—Dr Graham Dexter, Module Leader, University of Hull Coaching Masters Course

An excellent guide to assist organisations to help people reach a state where work becomes a healthy, balanced aspect of life, and the organisation grows as a sustainable creator of wealth.

—Dr Paul Donaldson, Chairman of Sysco Management Consultants Limited

This book presents a really useful challenge to every manager and leader, no matter how long they have been in business. I would recommend this to anyone brave enough to admit that they are now perfect!

—Suzanne Hughes, Regional Corporate Affairs Manager, Environment Agency – North West UK

I wish that I had access to this insightful book when I was a young manager who knew everything (!) but needed reference points and a counterview. Come to think of it, I wish that I'd had it when I was an old manager!

—Lawrence Jackson, Managing Director (retired), Gentech International Limited

Mike Wash is insightful, caring, realistic, and yet visionary. He wants you to make the best of the world and the people you find in it. If you believe in working together *healthily* for continuous improvement, then this book is for you. It tells you how to achieve it and how to spot mistakes you might be making. As ever, he writes clearly – with passion and yet with practicality. I wish he was my manager.

—Lindsey Jackson, Director, Enhance Wellbeing Limited

Having used the approaches described within this resource, and seen the benefits for individuals, teams, and the organisation as a result, I would say this is a must-have resource for any organisation development practitioner. Mike brings the subject matter to life in a very practical way.

—Alison Johnson, Assistant Director of Organisation Development, Halton and St Helens Primary Care Trust

Once again, Mike Wash provides telling insights from his great practical experience in identifying the symptoms shown by unhealthy organisations and guiding them towards a healthy future.

—Professor Tom McGuffog, MBE

Mike Wash is the kind of person who helps others to reach inside, find hidden resources, pull them, out and point them in the right direction, to produce great results in life and business. In this rich and accessible book, he helps the reader to understand the principles of how to work in an effective, an ethical, and a holistic way. If you work in any kind of human resources, you will want to read this book now!

—Dr Janice Russell, Module Leader, University of Hull Coaching Masters Course

This has all the most useful tools in the essential tool kit for someone new to the notion of manager as facilitator. This is essential organisational first aid to enable organisations to move towards greater health.

—Bryce Taylor, Director, Oasis School of Human Relations

54 Approaches to Organisational Healing is available at www.54.self-help-books.com

54 Steps to Happiness: How to Lose Weight by Realising What You Want

On this extraordinary journey, Mike Wash opens up his personal life to readers. In doing so, he challenges himself to become healthy in mind, body, and spirit. He uses his quest to lose weight as a vehicle to reflect on his life and, in doing so, challenges how we view others and the events around us. Written in 2005, it brings to life world events from that time period – from terrorism to major disasters – and therefore becomes one man's snapshot of history and a valuable record of our time for all to appreciate.

Included are the following:

The Journey of Happiness parable takes you on a journey of discovery and discovers the elements of happiness during encounters with mysterious figures and challenges.

The Wheel of Happiness is a useful graphic that brings together all the elements for effective living and reminds us of the ingredients of a well balanced and happy and fulfilling life.

Available at www.54-self-help-books.com.

5 + 4 = Sweet Dreams – Bedtime Stories for Three-to Nine-Year-Olds

What happens to a giant when he shrinks?

What could you do with a cloak that makes you invisible?

Could you be friends with a very ugly monster?

Imagine the reaction of your friends if you brought to school an alien from outer space.

Ever heard of a tiger that couldn't roar?

What if fairies did exist?

Imagine your toys coming alive!

How sad would a spotty dog be without spots?

What's it like being lost at a fairground?

The answers to these wonderful questions and more can be found in these easy-to-read bedtime (or anytime) stories.

The magic comes to life when the parent/guardian or teacher reads the stories to an audience of children whose eyes sparkle with inquisitive delight as they wait to find out what happens next! A sure way of nurturing imagination, early wisdom, and affection.

Available at www.54-self-help-books.com.